EXPLORING OSAKA

EXPLORING OSAKA
JAPAN'S SECOND CITY

DAVID M. DUNFIELD

NEW YORK • **WEATHERHILL** • TOKYO

First edition, 1993

Published by Weatherhill, Inc., 420 Madison Avenue, 15th Floor, New York, NY 10017. Protected by copyright under terms of the International Copyright Union; all rights reserved. Except for fair use in book reviews, no part of this book may be reproduced for any reason by any means, including any method of photographic reproduction, without permission of the publisher. Printed in the United States.

Photos by the author, except those credited otherwise

Library of Congress Cataloging in Publication Data

Dunfield, David M.
    Exploring Osaka / by David M. Dunfield.
       p.   cm.
    ISBN 0-8348-0271-6: $14.95
    1. Osaka (Japan)—Guidebooks. I. Title.
  DS897.0813D86   1993
  915.2'18340449—dc20   93-15656
                                                                    CIP

CONTENTS

vii	**PREFACE**
1	**HISTORY OF OSAKA**
9	**INSIDE THE LOOP**
11	UNDERGROUND UMEDA
17	OSAKA CASTLE AND VICINITY
24	THE RIVERFRONTS
33	OSAKA BUSINESS PARK
35	SHINSAIBASHI
39	NAMBA
45	SHITENNŌ-JI
49	UEMACHI RIDGE
51	TENNŌ-JI
69	**OUTSIDE THE LOOP**
71	SUMIYOSHI
76	HIRANO
79	SAKAI AND VICINITY
86	TONDABAYASHI CITY
89	KAWACHI NAGANO
100	OSAKA HARBOR
105	**NATURE**
107	PARKS
114	ESCAPING THE CITY
119	**DINING, SHOPPING, AND MORE**
121	SOURCES OF INFORMATION
123	DINING

128	HOTELS, INNS, AND HOSTELS
132	BOOKSTORES AND SPECIALTY SHOPPING
138	MUSEUMS AND ASSORTED MONUMENTS
145	FESTIVALS
149	**USEFUL KANJI**
157	**INDEX**
	ILLUSTRATIONS
55	MAPS
	PHOTOGRAPHS FOLLOWING PAGE 38

PREFACE

Osaka is not Japan's easiest city to love. In fact, for a city of its historical and economic importance, Osaka's place in the consciousness of visitors to Japan is remarkably small. Many of the thousands of foreigners who visit Osaka on business each year bring with them the image of a treeless, polluted, industrial wasteland, a sort of capitalist purgatory to be endured only as long as necessary.

Even among the Japanese, Osaka is often seen merely as a place in which to do business. There are historical reasons for Osaka's low standing in the Japanese consciousness. A canonical view of Japanese culture developed during the Meiji era (1868–1912) in which Kyoto and Nara were given the status of sources and centers of traditional culture, while Tokyo became the essence of modern society. Osaka, whose economic power during the preceding Edo (or Tokugawa) period (1615–1868) had been greatly resented—and quickly dismantled—by the new regime, was left out of the equation. In addition, some residue of the feudal class structure, in which merchants were at the bottom of the hierarchy, may continue to color the Japanese view of Osaka. Its people are sometimes characterized as miserly, selfish, and rude (though Osakans themselves might describe their traits as thrifty, individualistic, and candid).

Osaka's nicknames suggest its second-city status. As the "Rice Bowl of Japan" during the Edo period, Osaka's economic power was clearly stated. But the name also hints that while Japanese society was materially nourished by Osaka, the high cultural achievements of the ruling samurai class were produced elsewhere. At the beginning of the twentieth century, Osaka came to be known as the "Manchester of the East." Although this may have suggested industrial power and progressiveness to the city's promoters, it also calls to mind images of soot-blackened skies and dim, grimy factories. The most complimentary nickname for Osaka, the "Venice of Japan," was reported and possibly coined by an American geographer, Glenn Trewartha, in the 1930s. He had been impressed by the city's extensive network of canals, created in the Edo period and still in use prior to the Second

PREFACE

World War. But even Trewartha was quick to add that it was a very smoky Venice.

At certain times, in certain places, Osaka's environment can seem to confirm the worst of the bad press it has received. But the same can be said of any city in any part of the world. What you find is generally what you expected to find.

Up to now, English-speaking visitors have been given little reason to expect much from Osaka. Information in English on Osaka's historical, cultural, and scenic attractions is hard to come by. Bookstores which contain dozens of titles on Tokyo and Kyoto may sell none devoted to Osaka. English guides to Japan tend to mention only the most obvious monuments in their sections on Osaka. Travel writing which does focus on the city leans toward extremes—pollyannaish boosterism which paints even the most mediocre of sites in glowing rosy tones, or grouchy commentaries like the *New York Times* article on the Osaka Aquarium which opined that one of its best features was its convenience to public transportation, requiring the visitor to waste only half a day in the city on the aquarium tour.

I first lived in Osaka in the late 1970s. My wife, Pat, was pursuing a doctorate in the history of Japanese art and I was in the process of dropping out of the same field, in the throes of a premature midlife crisis. It was luck more than intention that brought us to Osaka, but we soon came to appreciate the city's special qualities and to realize the difficulty of finding English-language information on Osaka. The notion of writing a guide to the region dates from that experience.

After return visits to the city in the 1980s, we again took up residency in Osaka in 1991. While Pat conducted post-doctoral research in affiliation with Kansai University, I took on the role of full-time parent to our then seven-year-old son, Lee, and became an explorer of the city and prefecture.

All of the important sites are covered here, along with many that are less well known. I have tried to make the book informative, with historical data as well as logistical notes, but I have included personal impressions, opinions, and prejudices as well. The attractions I've written about, and the

PREFACE

editorial positions I take, are strongly colored by my background as a professional architect and an amateur art historian.

This is not a comprehensive guide by any means, but a compendium of favorite and otherwise memorable places. From isolated hiking trails to secluded medieval temples to state-of-the-art museums, Osaka is full of surprises, and it is a pleasure to share them.

Since I have not tried to create an all-inclusive guide, I have listed publications for English-speaking residents that deal with issues of daily living in Sources of Information (pages 121–22). I have provided maps for specific places discussed in the text; the major Japanese bookstores sell a number of maps and transportation system diagrams in English that give an overall view of Osaka.

I wish to acknowledge the considerable assistance of the following people: Professors Ōba Osamu and Kawamichi Rintarō of Kansai University; Ishii Osamu and my friends at Biken Architectural Design; Taki Mitsuo and Kozue; Heya Mitsuru and Kayoko; my wife, Pat Graham, whose knowledge and support were indispensable; and our son Lee, a good sport.

HISTORY OF OSAKA

HISTORY OF OSAKA

GEOGRAPHY A good place to start an introduction to the history of the Osaka region is its geography. Osaka's development has been strongly influenced throughout its history by several distinct geographic features. The land, however, has been so extensively modified in this century that many of those features have been obscured or obliterated. Thus, the events and monuments of Osaka's past are more comprehensible when seen in the context of the area's original physical setting.

Osaka's fortunes have been tied to the sea from its earliest origins to the present, and the physical changes to the coastline indicate the importance of the relationship. Osaka's current harbor is artificially constructed. It consists of deepwater ports created by dredging the sea bottom and by extending the shoreline into former sea through land reclamation projects. The old harbor was shallow and filled with shifting islands of sand and silt carried in from the Yamato and Yodo rivers. Old histories write of "80 Islands" in Osaka Bay. The harbor provided good anchorage for the small, shallow-draft boats used by the early inhabitants of the area, and became one of the country's most important early ports of entry.

The land around the harbor was, and still is, generally flat. The rivers feeding the harbor were not the swiftly flowing streams more typical of Japan, but were slow and meandering in their courses. In fact, tidal action turned much of the land immediately along the coast into salt marshes, fed alternately by fresh and salt water. Further east and south, the plain was higher. This land was more suited to agriculture, and particularly to growing rice, which requires diversion of large quantities of fresh water to flood fields during the growing season.

Rising out of this flat land is a low but distinct ridge running north-south from what is now the Osaka Castle site to Shitennō-ji. Although less than obvious in the densely developed city of today, this land formation—now known as Uemachi Ridge—would have dominated the landscape in early times. It became a sort of organizing element, a natural landmark along which the residents would build their own landmarks.

HISTORY OF OSAKA

PREHISTORY Japan's Neolithic culture, the Jōmon, and its successor, the Yayoi, both occupied the region which is now Osaka Prefecture. Jōmon remains are found throughout most of Japan, some dating as far back as ten thousand years ago. The Jōmon consisted of scattered tribes which had relatively little contact with one another. Yayoi culture, though covering a shorter time span, from roughly 200 B.C. to A.D. 250, represented a revolutionary change in the organization of Japanese culture. The basis for this revolution was the cultivation of rice, which was learned from immigrants from continental Asia. Yayoi culture began in Kyushu and spread north and east throughout much of Honshu. The many points of anchorage along the shores of Osaka Bay were no doubt employed by the Yayoi people, and a number of settlements have been identified in the area. The Yayoi, though sophisticated as farmers and as makers of pottery, and bronze and iron tools and weapons, were loosely organized politically.

It was the Yayoi people's successors who established the first unified kingdom in Japan, and Osaka's role during that period was central. The earliest Japanese histories, written in the seventh century A.D., describe the founding of the Japanese state by Emperor Jimmu. He is said to have sailed from the west (probably from Kyushu), and to have begun his battles against the local tribes at Naniwa, which is the oldest recorded place name for Osaka. (Naniwa means "rapid waves," and is still sometimes used by writers inclined toward the romantic.) After fighting for three years, he was able to establish Naniwa as his political center. While the date for this event given in the old histories is unrealistically early (660 B.C.) and some modern scholars even doubt the existence of Jimmu, archeological evidence supports the idea that Japan's first capital was indeed located in the Osaka area, around A.D. 400. This period is now referred to as the Kofun, or Tumulus, period (250–552), named for the burial mounds which are its most distinctive remains.

The largest and most famous of the thousands of Kofun burial mounds is found in Sakai, Osaka Prefecture. The mound is thought to be the resting place of Emperor Nintoku, and dates from the fifth century A.D. Its huge size is indicative of the concentration of power in the fledgling kingdom's center, while the presence of imported items among the burial goods suggests the continuing importance of Osaka's port as a trading center.

By the mid-sixth century political power had shifted inland, to the area around Asuka, Nara Prefecture. There the Yamato court would establish Japan's first literate era, the Asuka period (552–645).

EARLY HISTORY The Osaka region continued to play an important role in Japan's development after the political center shifted to Asuka and Nara. In addition to being a fishing community, the area was one of the country's two international ports, the other being in Kyushu. It makes sense that another early place name for Osaka is Tsu-no-kuni or "anchorage."

Three major monuments of this early historical period remain in Osaka today. The first, just south of the Osaka Castle grounds, is the excavated site of Naniwa Palace, constructed in 680 by Emperor Temmu. The site has been designated a national historical park, though no physical remains of the palace buildings are visible today. The stones placed, in modern times, over the locations of the original foundation stones give some sense of the scale of the palace, but little else. It is worth mentioning that the palace was situated precisely on the highest point of Uemachi Ridge. Naniwa Palace burned down in 683, but successive rulers built palaces in the same area until 745.

The other two monuments from the early historical period are Shitennō-ji and Sumiyoshi Taisha. Both are discussed more fully elsewhere in the book, but a brief mention here will suggest Osaka's status as Japan's "water capital." Sumiyoshi Taisha is among Japan's oldest shrines, dating to the late fourth or early fifth century A.D. Originally located just a few hundred meters from the sea—now the artificially extended shoreline increases that distance—it has been traditionally associated with mariners and fishermen. Shitennō-ji, the Buddhist temple founded in 593 by Prince Shōtoku, is east of the shrine on the southern end of Uemachi Ridge, where it served as an impressive landmark for visitors to the Japanese kingdom.

HISTORY OF OSAKA

THE MODERN CITY Osaka's development into a major city began in the mid-sixteenth century, a time of great social instability and frequent internal warfare. Local feudal lords acted autonomously, unrestrained by a weak central government. In this chaotic time, even Buddhist groups often became feudal powers, with their temples serving as fortifications as well as spiritual centers. One such temple was Hongan-ji, which was founded in 1490 by the monk Rennyo (eighth patriarch of his sect) and served as headquarters of the main branch of Pure Land Buddhism. The temple was originally located in Kyoto, but when the sect was driven out by rival forces, Shonyo, the group's tenth patriarch, moved the temple. The site he selected, in 1533, was at the north end of Uemachi Ridge (then called Ishiyama), near the ruins of Naniwa Palace, and the temple came to be called Ishiyama Hongan-ji.

The temple thrived and its political power grew, eventually encompassing whole provinces. A town developed around its headquarters, dependent on the temple for its economy and security. With its sizable population and strong defenses, Ishiyama Hongan-ji became in essence the capital of a self-governing religious state. But as such it became a target of Oda Nobunaga, a feudal lord then in the process of trying to subjugate the entire country to his rule. Nobunaga first attacked the temple fortress in 1570, but Hongan-ji managed to resist for a decade before finally surrendering. On the day of the surrender, the complex was burned, apparently by its former defenders as a last act of defiance. (Kyoto's famous Nishi Hongan-ji was established in 1591 as the successor to the Ishiyama headquarters, and remains the center of the Pure Land sect of Rennyo.)

Toyotomi Hideyoshi, a general under Nobunaga, recognized the site's strategic value, and began construction of Osaka Castle on the remains of Hongan-ji in 1581. When Nobunaga was assassinated in 1582, Hideyoshi succeeded him, and eventually realized the goal of bringing the country under military control. When his castle was completed in 1584, Osaka became the generalissimo's home base, the center of the country's military power. Hideyoshi died of an illness in 1598, and the power struggles began again. Hideyoshi's heirs, and his castle, fell to Tokugawa Ieyasu in the

Osaka Summer War of 1615. This event marked the beginning of the Tokugawa period, most commonly called the Edo period, a reference to the new capital. The Edo was a long period of internal peace and prosperity in which Osaka would play a major role.

As a means of maintaining his control, Hideyoshi had nationalized the distribution of staple goods. In essence, all the country's vital products were first delivered to Osaka, then shipped throughout the nation. This system made Osaka the bustling economic center of Japan. An extensive system of canals was built to facilitate the shipping of goods. A map of the city dating to 1683 (see last page of photographs, top) shows the canal system, the many bridges spanning the waterways, and the castle, rebuilt by the Tokugawa, overlooking the developing city. The Tokugawa shogunate continued Hideyoshi's distribution system, ensuring Osaka's economic dominance until the end of the Edo period in 1868.

Osaka's special place in the economy helped create its unique local character. Shogunal control of the city was relatively lenient, and Osakans became known for individualism and independence. Of 168 bridges in the city center during the Edo period, all but twelve were privately built and maintained. While the society as a whole observed a strict hierarchy of social classes (with merchants at the bottom), a group of Osakans established a private university, Kaitokudō, in 1726, which was open to all citizens, regardless of class. Trade activity led to intellectual exchanges as well, and Osaka became a center of both traditional and progressive learning, including the ideas filtering into the country from the West.

The Meiji Restoration of 1868 devastated the city's economy. Daimyo, the regional rulers under the Tokugawa system, had amassed huge debts with Osaka's merchants and bankers. Their debts were forgiven by the new central government, bankrupting many of the city's wealthiest families. The city's monopoly on the distribution of goods disappeared, permitting open competition which destroyed many more merchants.

Osaka rebuilt its economy as an industrial city, and soon led the country in industrial output. By the early years of the twentieth century, Osaka was again the economic center of Japan. In the Second World War its success once again made Osaka a prime target, this time for American bombers. The destruction of the central city during the raids of 1944 was nearly total, with only isolated pockets surviving.

The vicissitudes of modern development and of the war resulted in a geographical peculiarity which I have used in grouping the chapters that follow. The Japan Railways (JR) loop line, begun in 1895, encircles the most densely urbanized districts of the city; it is these districts which suffered most during the bombings. In general, then, the areas grouped under the heading "Inside the Loop" contain hardly any prewar monuments (Shitennō-ji and Osaka Castle count among the few), while districts "Outside the Loop" are those in which prewar remnants are most visible.

Once again risen from the ashes, Osaka today is a thoroughly modern metropolis. In recent decades, the city has hosted two major international expositions: the World Exposition of 1970 and the International Flower and Greenery Exposition of 1990. During the same period, the local government's emphasis has shifted from industrial development to improving the quality of life, and the city is visibly cleaner and greener than it was twenty years ago. A renewed commitment to the awareness and maintenance of Osaka's historical monuments is also in evidence, and quiet traces of the area's past exist alongside its lively contemporary structures.

INSIDE THE LOOP

WALHALLA CENTRAL HALL

UNDERGROUND UMEDA

Umeda today often feels like the center of Osaka, and for the commuter or the serious consumer, it does function as the city's downtown. Historically, though, Umeda is an upstart with a shady past. At the time of Hideyoshi's founding of the modern city, nearly all the land north of the island of Nakanoshima was a swampy and wooded waste, home perhaps to a few fishermen and struggling farmers. It became urbanized only after 1700, following completion of a civil engineering project to tame Shinji-gawa, one of Osaka's many extinct rivers. A district just north of Nakanoshima still carries the name Shinchi, literally "new land."

The area's early reputation was perhaps befitting a neighborhood grown from a swamp. It became one of Osaka's pleasure districts, and accounts suggest that it was not of the most refined sort. In fact, the Umeda-Sonezaki area was best known in the Edo period as the setting for Osaka's most famous love suicide, a historical event adapted by Chikamatsu Monzaemon, the Osaka dramatist universally regarded as Japan's greatest.

The Love Suicides at Sonezaki, the tale of the prostitute Ohatsu and her lover Tokubei, is among the most famous Bunraku dramas in Japanese literature. The lovers are forced to keep their relationship clandestine, to avoid the scandal that would ensue if Ohatsu's customers and Tokubei's employer—who is trying to arrange his marriage—were ever to find out. The two resolve to overcome these obstacles, but Tokubei is swindled by another merchant and left penniless and in disgrace, with no honorable exit under the codes of the day except suicide. In the play's most dramatic scene, Ohatsu declares their intention to die together to the swindler while Tokubei hides under the teahouse veranda.

The play is filled with familiar place names, but Shinji-gawa—upon whose banks the lovers end their lives—is no more. A shrine associated with the events still exists (in the form of a postwar concrete building), and is generally known by its nickname, Ohatsu Tenjin, rather than the original, Tsuyu Tenjin. Even the central Sonezaki entertainment arcade is named in her honor. Running north-south and located east of Higashi Umeda Station,

UNDERGROUND UMEDA

Ohatsu-tenjin-dōri is typical of the less fashionable entertainment arcades of Umeda, where the evenings are filled with drunken laughter and the solicitations of barkers outside bars that feature photos of the scantily clad hostesses, Ohatsu's modern-day successors. The actual shrine can be found at the south end of Ohatsu-tenjin-dōri.

Umeda's transformation into the center which it is today began with the establishment of Osaka Station in 1874. As the Kansai district's industry and transportation systems developed, the private railways, Hankyu and Hanshin, added their own terminals adjacent to Osaka Station. Finally, the Osaka subway brought three lines into the district, one of them terminating at Umeda. The result is Osaka's busiest, most complicated locus in the commuter web, a hair-raising rush-hour maze bordered by a bewildering abundance of shops and restaurants capable of trapping all but the most single-minded or jaded of travelers.

At street level, gridlock is a way of life. A co-worker late for an appointment once convinced me to share his cab, and a 10-minute walk became a 20-minute ride. Crossing major streets requires either admirable patience or agility, or a willingness to climb the many artificial peaks of pedestrian overpasses. The ingenious remedy to the congestion of the Umeda area was simply to build another Umeda—underground.

Had underground Umeda been planned, it would have been a tremendous leap of the imagination, and a belief in the limitless adaptability of human consciousness, that devised this solution. Below the streets is a city devoid of all contact with sun and weather, in which distant landmarks are inconceivable and solitude impossible—in short, an environment in which most traditional sources of physical and psychic orientation are absent. Of course, underground Umeda was not really designed. It no doubt began as a few passages connecting train stations and only gradually acquired a life of its own, like a Frankenstein monster growing spontaneously from the spare-parts bin.

If I sound unenthusiastic, it is true that I hope Umeda does not represent the urban future, of Japan or the world. Still, it is a unique and fascinating

UNDERGROUND UMEDA

place, and one that would be extremely hard to avoid when traveling around or through Osaka. It should also be noted that underground Umeda is generally a more convenient place than the above-ground version: it's free of smog, temperate and dry in all seasons, clogged only with pedestrians (rarely as hazardous as BMWs), and packed with all the requisite amenities from noodle counters to Gucci outlets.

For those not bothered by claustrophobia, underground Umeda's major drawback is its complexity, amplified by the lack of those elements which give our subconscious minds a sense of place and direction. Being lost in Umeda is an experience shared by all who venture there, Japanese as well as foreign, and I would not wish to deprive anyone of this opportunity to form an emotional bond with fellow explorers. Nonetheless, it is an experience one doesn't ask to repeat too frequently. For that reason I have developed what I believe is the only reasonably complete map of underground Umeda in English (map 1); it may be the most useful bit of information in this book. You might want to mark your copy with personal landmarks and destinations (for example, Shakey's Pizza is one block north of the northeast exit from Whity East).

The map indicates the major shopping areas, rail stations, and passageways interconnected beneath Umeda's streets. Although I have shown about 8 kilometers of corridors, the total must be more than twice that. Those familiar with the Hankyu Sanbangai complex will immediately recognize that I have greatly simplified its layout. My intention has been to record the major routes taken while negotiating the maze, not to show every branch serving every cluster of shops. Moreover, some of the areas are multistoried, requiring additional simplification—I have not distinguished between levels on the map. Again using the example of Sanbangai, the two points of connection between it and Puchishan Mall occur on the second level down, B2, while the link to the north end of Midōsuji Line Umeda Station is on B1.

With these explanations behind us, it is time to take the plunge, map firmly in hand. Starting at the north we find the aforementioned Hankyu

UNDERGROUND UMEDA

Sanbangai, the flashiest, least subterranean-feeling portion of the buried city. This complex features two underground levels of shopping, with north and south "pavilions." The north end houses Kiddieland, a toy store of stunning size with everything from Hello Kitty to replica assault rifles, not to mention the ever-popular voice-activated beer cans. A two-story space just south of Kiddieland contains Water Circus Aqua Magic, a computerized fountain with precision jets of water leaping around a pond and jumping through hoops like trained seals in an ever-changing choreography. In the link connecting north and south areas is Space Tunnel, an environmental sculpture which I would liken to an abstract rainstorm in light and sound. From here on Sanbangai gets down to the serious business of selling food (Gourmet Museum, level B2) and clothing (Fashion Museum, level B1). Water displays, open spaces, and sculptures are also found here, but their impact is considerably diluted by the opulent storefronts and displays. For Americans accustomed to enclosed shopping malls, Sanbangai is not such an alien environment—all it really lacks is a skylight or two.

At roughly the southwest corner of Sanbangai (level B1) is a corridor connected to the north end of Midōsuji Line Umeda Station. Continuing west as far as possible, an exit leads up to Osaka Station—the easiest among the many connections between the Midōsuji and JR lines. Midway down Umeda Station another corridor heads east across the north end of Hankyu department store, but does not give access to it, skimming on by Osaka Grand Building until ending at the juncture between two shopping malls—Puchishan to the north and Whity North to the south.

Whity Mall is the absurdly named hub of underground Umeda, and consists of central, south, east, and two north divisions. From Whity Central spin off the entrances to the Hankyu and Hanshin department stores, the south entrance to the Midōsuji Line Umeda Station, the east entrance to the Hanshin Line Umeda Station, and the north entrance to the Tanimachi Line Higashi Umeda Station. It is also the river into which pour the tributaries Whity North (both malls 1 and 2), Whity South, and the mighty Whity East.

West of the Whity agglomeration begins Hanshin territory. Hanshin Mall consists of an attenuated line of individually operated stalls featuring *omiyage* (souvenirs) from around the country. The atmosphere is strictly bargain basement. Conveniently located near the Osaka Station, Hanshin Mall provides emergency gifts for returning travelers too absent-minded or overburdened to stock up before heading for home. In the midst of the souvenirs a corridor branches north, directly under ACTY Osaka and Osaka Terminal Hotel, and up to the Osaka Station central entrance. Further west along Hanshin Mall is another such branch; this one leads to the station's west entrance and is also the most convenient route to the Central Post Office. At this point, the passageways take a somewhat confusing turn, with one branch ending at Hanshin Hotel, another turning back to the west entrance of the Hanshin Line Umeda Station, and a third leading to the Yotsubashi Line Nishi Umeda Station.

Following the latter to the south, the passage again expands and becomes the Dōjima shopping arcade, which finally terminates just a block north of Nakanoshima. Dōjima is a rather nondescript arcade, sort of an underground version of your neighborhood *shōtengai* (shopping street).

Returning to the south end of Nishi Umeda Station, the Osaka Ekimae complex branches off to the east. The four buildings which make up this group are interconnected at the basement level. Primarily office space above ground, the two underground levels are occupied by retail shops and restaurants. The Ekimae restaurants are mostly lunch counters for the office workers, and the retailing is similarly unpretentious. Actually, there are some unusual stores (a jazz record shop, for example) and a sort of flea-market quality about the place that distinguishes it from the rest of underground Umeda. The northernmost of the Ekimae buildings, number 4, connects to the south end of Higashi Umeda Station.

From here, it's a short hop north to the Whity South mall. For the sake of thoroughness you can wrap back around to the southwest and visit the Shin Hankyu Building, with its small cluster of shops on the B1 level and restaurants on B2.

At street level, and above it all the way to the observation and dining levels of Hankyu 32 Bangai, Umeda's character is still overwhelmingly commercial. One women's clothing chain has at least four outlets within a 5-minute walk of Whity Central. The architecture of the area is largely unexceptional. The Umeda bookstores and galleries, and a sampling of restaurants and hotels, are listed in the final section of this guide: Dining, Shopping, and More.

OSAKA CASTLE AND VICINITY

Osaka Castle is without doubt the city's most compelling landmark. Its location on the highest ground in the city was chosen for purposes of symbolism as well as defense, and has served the former function well, even as the city's modern skyline has developed ever more and higher peaks. The nearby towers of the Osaka Business Park, for all their glittering acrobatics, do not overpower the castle, with its massive stone walls spreading concentrically from the monumental pyramidal form of the central structure, the donjon.

The castle is easily reached by rail from the JR Osaka-jō Kōen or Morinomiya stations, or by subway from the Tanimachi 4-chōme, Morinomiya, or Temmabashi stations.

Osaka Castle was, in its brief time of glory, the largest and most elaborate of Japan's castles. Toyotomi Hideyoshi chose the site with the intention of making it the center of a Japanese nation unified under his military rule. However, it served its intended role only from the time of its completion in 1584 until the Tokugawa overthrew Hideyoshi's son and successor in 1615.

Toyotomi Hideyoshi was an imposing character, a commoner who rose to the pinnacle of power in a society where upward social mobility was nearly unknown. His parents had planned a life in the Buddhist priesthood for the young Hiyoshimaru, as he was originally named, but he ran away from home at the age of fifteen and entered the service of the daimyo at Kuno. Not content with this provincial location, he bought armor and weapons with money entrusted to him by his master and fled to the headquarters of Oda Nobunaga, initially using a false name to hide his background.

Nobunaga was quick to see unusual talent in the young man, promoted him rapidly through the ranks, and bestowed the name by which he is now known. As a general under Nobunaga, Toyotomi Hideyoshi compiled a string of battlefield successes and was rewarded with ever larger and more important landholdings. When Nobunaga was assassinated in 1582, Hideyoshi's troops defeated and killed the assassins' faction. He then expected to be named Nobunaga's successor, but was opposed by the Oda clan. Over the next two years, Hideyoshi consolidated his power through a series of battlefield and diplomatic maneuvers, becoming the uncontested leader of the country by the time of the castle's completion in 1584. The title of shogun, or "commander-in-chief," was denied him due to his low social class, but the emperor conferred upon him the title *kampaku,* "chief minister," in 1586.

Hideyoshi was a volatile personality, known for his generosity and his patronage of the arts but capable of seemingly arbitrary, almost casual, cruelty. Hideyoshi's biography is full of anecdotes reflecting the contradictions in his character. He practiced the stringent rituals of the tea ceremony, carried out in an atmosphere of self-conscious poverty, and threw lavish parties in which he invited the whole population of Kyoto to share tea with him. The great tea master Sen no Rikyū developed his classic style of tea ceremony under Hideyoshi's patronage. Yet later in Hideyoshi's life, as he became increasingly unstable, he ordered Rikyū to commit suicide. One account says he was miffed at the tea master's refusal to give his daughter to Hideyoshi as a concubine.

Hideyoshi died in 1598, leaving a council of five generals to rule on behalf of his son Hideyori, then just five years old. The plan failed, and one of the three, Tokugawa Ieyasu, finally emerged victorious in the warfare that followed, which culminated in the destruction of Osaka Castle in 1615. Hideyori and his mother, Yodo-gimi, were among those who died in the conflagration.

In fact, the site has suffered more than its share of disasters, beginning even before Hideyoshi's time. As discussed in the history chapter, Hideyoshi first had to dislodge the religious/military complex of Ishiyama Hongan-ji before he could establish his own fortress there. The Hongan-ji complex was itself as much castle as temple, and Hideyoshi's builders probably incorporated remains of the old fortifications into the new design, though no traces have been identified. After the Osaka Summer War of 1615, the victorious Tokugawa forces razed all the buildings of the castle complex, leaving only the stone walls and moats. Beginning in 1619 the Tokugawa rebuilt the castle as a regional fortress, though the new donjon was considerably smaller and less lavish than Hideyoshi's. The new donjon also had a brief life—it was destroyed by lightning in 1665. The remainder of the complex survived the long reign of the Tokugawa, only to be heavily damaged again during the Meiji Restoration of 1868, when symbols of the old feudal order were attacked throughout the country.

Today's donjon is a reinforced concrete reconstruction based on paintings of Hideyoshi's original fortress, and is as accurate in scale and exterior form as possible given the evidence available. (Some claim that the original was as much as 25 percent larger than the reconstruction, but that opinion may derive more from Hideyoshi's larger-than-life reputation than from any clear evidence.) The concrete castle was built in 1931 using funds donated by the citizens of Osaka, reflecting both civic pride and the growing fervor of imperialism. In fact, the site's strategic and symbolic value was recognized by the Imperial Army, which established its 4th Division Headquarters adjacent to the donjon in the same year. Both the donjon and the headquarters building managed to survive the war, in spite of the site's military significance and its high visibility as a target. The former Division Headquarters is now the City Museum.

Despite its calamitous history, the remains of Osaka Castle continue to top the list of stops on any tour of the city, and with good reason. The castle complex is still a magnificent monument, deserving of at least a half-day's exploration. Other sights in the immediate vicinity include the Osaka Business Park (see pages 33–34) and the remains of Naniwa Palace.

Naniwa Palace is the oldest excavated historical site in the city, and is especially significant to local pride as it established Osaka as the imperial residence during a portion of the seventh century. As a result, it appears in many tour guides and itineraries. However, the site itself is a disappointment in that none of the actual excavations or remains are on view. They have been reburied, with the locations of building foundations marked by stones or other modern structures which convey little sense of the original palace and even less of the process by which it was rediscovered and studied.

A tour of Osaka Castle properly starts among the tour buses and colored pennants outside the Ōte-mon, the main gate to the complex, built in 1629. Follow the signs from Tanimachi 4-chōme (the nearest subway station) to Ōte-mon. You may wish to find a gap between tour groups, making a special effort to avoid the swarms of uniformed schoolchildren. The intimidating scale of the castle is immediately evident here. Massive wooden doors on gargantuan iron hinges and vast stone walls still elicit awe.

Inside the Ōte-mon is the first of several huge stones that have been carefully cut and placed into the fortification's walls at locations clearly chosen to make the greatest impact on visitors. Throughout the castle complex, the stone masonry is skillfully cut and set without mortar in a style unmatched elsewhere in Japan. I visited the mountainside (now an expensive housing district) in Nishinomiya, Hyōgo Prefecture, where stones for the castle were quarried. Many still project from the ground on the upper reaches of the mountain—some showing marks from stonecutters' tools of centuries ago—in shape and color clearly cousins of those in the castle walls. The extraction and transportation of these stones, first down the mountainside, then by ship across Osaka Bay, and finally upriver to the castle site, was an undertaking worthy of the ego and ambition of Hideyoshi.

Beside the Ōte-mon stands the Tamon Turret of 1620, the oldest of the several *yagura* (turrets) that remain from the Edo-period rebuilding of the castle. The Tamon Turret takes the form of a second gate, requiring intruders to pass under openings from which stones could be dropped or through which weapons could be fired. Similar openings in the other turrets at Osaka Castle are clearly visible as projected sections of wall, but those in the Tamon Turret are concealed. All the turrets were constructed out of wood, so fireproofing their exteriors was a primary consideration. This was achieved by building up a thick layer of mud-based plaster covering all exposed wood surfaces. The combination of plaster and ceramic tile roofs made the turrets relatively secure from attack in a time when heavy artillery was unavailable. And it is the construction techniques developed for turrets that define the appearance of Japanese castles.

A total of five turrets from the Edo period remain at the castle site, and deserve a close look, since it is only in these small structures that the construction methods and details employed in the original donjon can still be seen. Unfortunately, none of the turrets' interiors are open to the public, except for a few days each spring and autumn.

Immediately before you as you pass through the Tamon Turret is a large area between the inner and outer moats called the Nishinomaru. This area contains several interesting buildings and is generally less crowded than the inner section of the grounds, permitting a more leisurely viewing of the structures. To the left is the Sengan Turret, which is more typical in form than the Tamon Turret. It is a simple square in plan, perched on a corner of the wall overlooking the outer moat. Further north is the Inui Turret, which is L-shaped in plan. Finally, at the north end of the Nishinomaru is the most unusual building in the castle complex. This is the Enshō-gura, or Gunpowder Storehouse, and its construction eloquently expresses its purpose. Where the turrets are wooden and covered in clay, and thus only moderately safe from destruction by fire, the Enshō-gura is built entirely of granite. The walls are massive, the building's form squat and compact. There are no windows, just a door at each end. Even the tile roof is supported on a framework of stone—a unique structure in Japan, which has no tradition of masonry vaulting like that in the West. The massiveness of the building makes it appear not only capable of protecting its contents against attack, but also of containing an explosion within its walls.

Leaving the Nishinomaru, you approach the Sakura-mon, a gate reconstructed in 1872. Beyond the gate the stonework is particularly impressive, and includes the largest stone in the complex, nicknamed the Octopus. You have now entered the Honmaru, the inner courtyard of Osaka Castle and nerve center of the city's tourist industry. Stop to admire the donjon once more while you are still far enough away to imagine that it is the genuine article—close inspection will forever shatter that illusion. The scale and the rhythmic interplay of the roof projections are real enough, as is the sense of authoritarian power.

Making your way through the clutter of souvenir stands and food stalls, you finally reach the donjon, buy your ticket and enter, only to discover another souvenir stand, concrete floors and ubiquitous arrows leading to the most unexpected feature of all, an elevator. Since you've come this far, you may as well enjoy the view from the castle's top. (It's the best vantage point in Osaka, in my opinion. High enough to provide sweeping vistas but still in contact with the earth, it continues to feel—despite all modern aggregations—like the historic locus of the city.) Displays in the galleries on the way back down are of mixed quality, but include some excellent photographs, drawings, and scale models of the castle and the excavations and reconstructions related to it.

The other focus of attention in the Honmaru is the City Museum, a peculiar structure modeled in a halfhearted way on medieval European castles, complete with crenellated parapets. As previously noted, this was originally designed as an Imperial Army headquarters; the combination of Western style (implying modern technology and strength) with the historic castle site apparently led the architect into strange territory, with unfortunate results. The museum's collection is of a higher caliber than its building, featuring information about Osaka's development and including a good number of archeological artifacts from around the city. Remains from the Naniwa Palace, conspicuously absent at the palace site, are on view here. The museum also hosts special exhibitions, usually of artwork associated with the city's history.

The perimeter of the Honmaru is worth walking around; it provides good views and shady picnic spots. For another perspective on the castle, exit the Honmaru to the north, then turn east into Osaka-jō Kōen. This large but undistinguished park contains athletic fields, an amphitheater, a wooded grove, and a peculiar plum grove (*bairin*) with a myriad of twisting paths. At the north end of the park is Osaka-jō Hall, a 16,000-seat multi-use arena. This huge hall has been designed with surprising sensitivity to the castle's context. It makes use of some elements borrowed from the castle—stone masonry and copper roofing—without any futile attempt at matching or blending with the castle's style. The architects have also handled the hall's size effectively, giving the building a low profile, with stone walls suggestive of terraces spreading out from the hall and thus merging its edges with the landscape.

OSAKA CASTLE AND VICINITY

Another attraction closely related to the castle is the Aqualiner, a sightseeing boat whose tours depart from a landing northwest of Osaka-jō Hall. The hour-long tour cruises the rivers overlooked by the castle, and thus reinforces the vital importance of the rivers (and the many now-defunct canals that branched off from them) as medieval Osaka's transportation network. The tour provides another perspective not only on the castle but also on the riverfronts north to the Osaka Mint and west along both shores of Nakanoshima, some of Osaka's most memorable urban scenery.

Leaving the castle environs means re-entering today's more efficient if less romantic mass transit system: about 600 meters east of the Aqualiner landing is Osaka-jō Kōen Station on the JR loop line.

OSAKA CASTLE GROUNDS   Always open. Admission: free.

DONJON   9 A.M. to 8:30 P.M. from July 15 to August 31; 9 A.M. to 5 P.M. during the rest of the year. Admission: ¥400.

NISHINOMARU   9 A.M. to 5 P.M. Closed Mondays. Admission: ¥150.

CITY MUSEUM   9:15 A.M. to 4:45 P.M. Closed the second and fourth Monday of every month. Admission: ¥200.

AQUALINER   10 A.M. to 5 P.M. Additional cruises at 6 P.M. and 7 P.M. from April 1 to September 30, and also at 8 P.M. from July 15 to August 31. Admission: ¥1,600.

THE RIVERFRONTS

Along the riverfronts north and west of the castle are some of Osaka's finest urban scenes. This area was the northern edge of the city in Edo times, when Umeda was but a remote and gloomy suburb. The island of Nakanoshima (literally, "center island") and the districts flanking it developed as a business district early in the seventeenth century. In 1619, the Tokugawa government ordered Yodoya Jōan, the most prominent Osaka merchant of the day, to build warehouses for rice and other goods on the island. By 1700, there were ninety-five daimyo rice warehouses in Osaka, most of them on or alongside Nakanoshima. The local daimyo throughout Japan sent their tax payments, in the form of rice, to these warehouses. Osaka merchants acted as middlemen, receiving and storing the payments on behalf of the government. In the process, the merchants prospered and expanded their sphere of activities. Their wealth allowed them to undertake major public works projects, such as the building of bridges and canals. Osaka merchants also invented the practice of lending money to land-rich but cash-poor daimyo, a practice which would contribute to the merchants' downfall at the end of the Tokugawa rule, when all such debts were cancelled by the new Meiji government.

The Meiji Restoration of 1868 made the trading district obsolete, and the area was rapidly transformed into a government and business center, intended to be a model of the Western institutional style. Foreign architects and Japanese trained in European academies were commissioned to create an appropriate environment for these new institutions, and such innovative amenities as public parks and promenades were woven into the urban fabric. Thankfully, many of the stone and brick structures built during the Meiji era remain, as does much of their surrounding context of streets, parks, and bridges. This district, which includes Nakanoshima, Sakuranomiya Park, and the Osaka Mint, proves that, contrary to popular belief, Osaka has gracious urban spaces and a distinctive character.

In my own exploration of Osaka, I returned frequently to this area to enjoy the seasonal changes in the parks, to revisit and sketch favorite views, and simply to watch the barges on the rivers and the traffic flowing on the bridges that cross the water. For the sake of those with less time to spend, I have designed a full day's sightseeing tour that covers the high points (see map 2). Since there are few restaurants along the path, and much of the tour involves being outdoors in parks and promenades, picnic lunches are very much in order.

The first stage begins at the northern end of the district at Sakuranomiya Station on the JR loop line. About a hundred meters south of the station is an entrance to Sakuranomiya Park, which extends southward along the east bank of the Yodo River and along the west bank south of Sakuranomiya-bashi. A quiet park favored by retirees playing bocce, dog walkers, and siesta takers, it has a total length of over 4 kilometers. About 1.2 kilometers south of your point of entry into the park, turn west and cross Sakuranomiya-bashi. This iron bridge was constructed in 1930 and is a splendid example of the industrial style of its time.

After crossing the bridge, a short path on the north side of Highway 1 leads back another half century in time, to two buildings of the early Meiji era. Both were constructed as part of the original Osaka Mint, Japan's first producer of modern coinage. The architectural style was imported along with the production techniques and the machinery itself.

The two buildings of the Osaka Mint were designed in the period from 1868 to 1871 by Thomas Waters, a British surveyor-architect who was among the first to bring foreign styles to Japan. The finest of the buildings is the Sempu-kan, designed as a guest house for important visitors to the Mint. Among its early guests was none other than the Meiji Emperor, who bestowed its rather prosaic name, which means "House of Currency." The style of the structure is something of a surprise—a British colonial house that would seem more at home in Calcutta, complete with a veranda on three sides at both the first and second levels, and shuttered doors to the outside from every room. It is a style suited to warm, humid weather, of which Osaka certainly has its share for part of the year. Like traditional Japanese design, comfort in summer was given a higher priority than winter warmth. The Sempu-kan is a design modest in detail but stately and dignified in overall appearance.

THE RIVERFRONTS

The Sempu-kan's companion piece is made up of a stone facade (the main entrance portal of the original Mint complex) applied to a later structure. It is a rather dry and awkward exercise in Greco-Roman style, with curious circular figures, perhaps coins, in the pediment. A designated Important Cultural Property, its importance is due to its early date among Western-style masonry buildings in Japan and not to any aesthetic merit. The building behind the facade now houses exhibitions of children's artwork, much of which is considerably livelier than the building.

Across Highway 1 to the south is the Mint itself. The bulk of the Mint is off limits to the public, and security is understandably strict; attempts to wander are met by polite but strict rebuffs from white-gloved and white-helmeted guards. There is a museum on the grounds, however, and after picking up a pass at the security office you can walk unaccompanied along the prescribed paths to reach it. The Mint Museum contains a fine collection of ancient and modern coins from around the world, with a special emphasis, of course, on those of Japan and East Asia. The large ovals of hammered gold produced during Hideyoshi's time are especially beautiful. The history of the Osaka Mint and the process of modern coin-making are subjects of other well-produced displays. A larger portion of the Mint grounds is open for two weeks each year during cherry-blossom season, and is mobbed with visitors seeking the ultimate floral experience among the Mint's diverse collection of cherry-tree varieties. My recommendation is that you visit the museum during the week before or after the cherry-blossom viewing—the trees will be in a less than ideal state, but they will at least be visible.

Walking south from the Mint along the west bank of the Yodo River takes you through a promenade also lined with cherry trees. Except when the cherries are in bloom, this stretch of Sakuranomiya Park is a peaceful haven for a midday stroll. However, if you have never experienced a full-blown Japanese cherry-blossom-viewing event, this is the place in Osaka to do so. The boisterous, densely packed throng, eating bento (box lunches), drinking sakè, and singing traditional songs (accompanied by karaoke machines)—all in the name of appreciating one of nature's most fragile and subtle blossoms—is a sight that every foreign visitor should experience.

The next bridge south of Sakuranomiya-bashi is Kawasaki-bashi, a pedestrians-only structure completed in 1978. This bridge also derives its aesthetic appeal from its structural system. In this case, the structure is a sophisticated and delicate span supported by cables suspended from a single, asymmetrical pylon. The contrast between this bridge and the 1930 span upriver is a striking comment on the evolution of engineering over a fifty-year interval.

After crossing the bridge, a 5-minute walk to the northeast will bring you to the Fujita Museum of Art. The collection formerly belonged to Baron Fujita Denzaburō, who made a fortune as a leader in the industrialization of Osaka during the Meiji era. His residence, on the site of the museum, was largely destroyed during the Second World War. The museum is comprised of the storehouses, which survived the war. Across the street from the museum is the restaurant Taikō-en (see page 125). Taikō-en's grounds were also part of the Fujita estate and its banquet halls, like the museum's buildings, are survivors of the war.

The Fujita Museum's facilities are modest in appearance but contain one of Japan's finest collections of Oriental art. The museum is closed several months each year, so confirm that it is open before making the trek. There are only two small galleries, so only a tiny portion of the collection is on view at any one time, and there is an unusually high admission charge. Nevertheless, the quality of the pieces makes the trip worthwhile. Also on the museum grounds are a small, delicately detailed pagoda which originally stood on Mt. Kōya, and a beautiful teahouse and garden. The latter are often closed to the public, but you may be able to persuade the staff to open them to you for a private viewing.

After returning to and recrossing Kawasaki-bashi, the next bridge to the west along the river is Tenjin-bashi, which crosses the eastern tip of Nakanoshima, the island that is the heart of Osaka's remaining vestiges of prewar modernization. This end of the island is Nakanoshima Kōen, established as Osaka's first city park in 1890. Its layout is decidedly Western in style, with large lawns, benches overlooking the rivers, and a Victorian-style rose garden. The park is diligently maintained, though the two bridges which cross it provide shelters for the homeless, an unhappy sight, but certainly no danger to the visitor's safety.

At the west end of the park is Naniwa-bashi, whose monumental stairs, antique streetlights, and carved stone lions make a dignified entrance to the park and a good starting point for an exploration of Nakanoshima's streets and buildings. The first building east of Naniwa-bashi is the Museum of Oriental Ceramics, which opened in 1982 to house the world-famous Ataka Collection, donated to the city by the Sumitomo companies. Like the Fujita Museum collection, the Ataka Collection is a testament to the taste and the wealth of a Meiji-era industrialist. The facility reflects the art on display, stylish but not trendy, memorable without upstaging the exquisite pieces. A computer-controlled skylight illuminates some of the finest pieces in muted daylight so that their colors can be seen as their makers intended. I was flabbergasted to discover on my first visit to the museum that my three favorite works from the history of Chinese ceramic art were all in the permanent display. Special exhibits are held several times a year.

West of the museum are several early-twentieth-century buildings that demonstrate the Japanese assimilation of Western ideas and techniques following the Meiji Restoration. First is the Nakanoshima Central Hall of 1918, a grand and eccentric structure. Its designer, Okada Shin'ichirō, was among the first generation of European-trained Japanese architects. The architectural elements of the building are individually conservative, but their fanciful combination resulted in a lively ensemble, especially at the main entrance. There, a large arched opening is oddly subdivided by classical columns whose capitals are lopsided to receive the curving surface; the arch presses outward against towers whose stubby, stone-cornered forms seem to resist it doggedly. Within, the building contains a large central space originally intended as a ballroom but now used for more prosaic gatherings. The once grand space is in need of restoration.

The Central Hall's neighbor to the west is the Osaka Prefectural Library. Another Japanese architect trained in the Western style, Noguchi Magoichi, designed the central portion of the library in 1904, with additions in 1915 and 1922. The building's style is Roman Revival, with a central dome and a

Corinthian-columned portico. Though it lacks the exuberance of the Central Hall, the central space under the dome is an attractive one, somewhat cluttered in its present state with card catalogues and information desks. For scholars, the library is one of Osaka's prime attractions. Its collection is superb, especially in the areas of regional history and culture.

Beginning at the Museum of Oriental Ceramics, and continuing past the Central Hall and the library, the island is provided with generous pedestrian walkways, giving it a friendly quality sorely lacking in so many modern cities the world over. The walkways continue in the form of a promenade along both the north and south edges of Nakanoshima. Along the north side is Suishō-bashi, a muscular, Romanesque pedestrian span which is most attractive when lit at night. Continuing to the west, you pass the Osaka City Hall and arrive at the Bank of Japan buildings. The older of the bank structures was designed in 1903 by Tatsuno Kingō, perhaps the most famous Japanese architect who practiced in premodern European styles. Tatsuno's building is neo-Rennaissance, executed with a confidence and ease one might expect from an architect of his stature. In fact, the building is quite similar in composition and detail to the much larger Bank of Japan which Tatsuno designed for the home branch in Tokyo a decade earlier. Behind the original structure is an addition by Nikken Sekkei, dating to 1982. The addition maintains a respectful distance from the original, but still establishes its own strong identity. The large, modern building also respects the pedestrian scale of the promenades—low and horizontal at the street edges, it rises in a series of articulated steps to a massive form set well back into the block.

Before moving on to the west, a detour both in space and time is in order. Between the Bank of Japan and City Hall is Yodoya-bashi. Cross it to the south and continue a block south and two east to find Osaka city's oldest remaining *machiya* (townhouse), built in the last decade of the eighteenth century. Tekijuku, as the house is known, would be valuable simply as a historical artifact, since few premodern domestic structures survive in Osaka, but its primary importance is due to the individual who bought the house and occupied it in 1843. Ogata Kōan was the son of a samurai family

THE RIVERFRONTS

who, at the age of seventeen, developed an interest in Western learning which he would pursue for the rest of his life. Although only a few Dutch traders were allowed in Japan at the time, and those few were restricted to Dejima Island in Nagasaki, Western ideas and materials did circulate around the country, especially in major trading centers such as Osaka. Kōan studied first in Osaka, then in Edo (Tokyo), and finally in Nagasaki, where he learned Western medicine. Returning to Osaka, he established his own school of Western learning called Tekijuku, which might be translated as "Proper Learning." The school enrolled fifty students at a time, many of whom resided in the building, which was also Kōan's house. The school was coeducational, a policy as radical as its curriculum. The primary subject was the Dutch language, then considered by Kōan and other Japanese students of the West to be the key to unlocking the secrets of Western science, technology, and culture. Their primary reference book was a single, handwritten, eight-volume Dutch-Japanese dictionary, still displayed in the room where it was kept and used.

Kōan was famous in his time for his medical knowledge; the efficacy of Western medicine was recognized even by the intensely xenophobic Tokugawa ruling family. In fact, Kōan was ordered, in 1862, to become the official physician to the Tokugawa family, and moved back to Edo. Some of his students, however, became too outspoken in urging that Japan open to the West, and one, Hashimoto Sanai, was executed by the shogunate. Among the school's other alumni were several influential scholars and physicians, including the founders of both Keio University and the Japanese Red Cross.

Tekijuku today is in splendid condition thanks to a 1978 restoration project. Sandwiched among high-rise office buildings, it is a surprising sight: a typical Edo-period merchant house with mud-plastered walls, wooden lattice shutters, and tile roof. Inside, the first floor is also typical of a *machiya*. Along the west side, behind the entrance door, is a series of dirt-floored rooms, a combination of *genkan* (entrance hall), storeroom, and kitchen. A series of tatami rooms used as classrooms by Kōan but originally intended as a merchant's shop take up the front of the east side. Next is a tiny courtyard garden, followed by the family's living quarters, which culminate in a large guest room that faces a larger garden. Beyond, at the south end of the compound are a *kura* (storehouse) and a toilet, the former detached for reasons of safety in case of fire, the second for sanitary reasons.

The upper level in a typical machiya would have been unfinished attic space. Kōan had this space expanded and finished to provide a dormitory for his students. It consists of three rooms; the largest was the male students' sleeping room, followed by a room where the Dutch-Japanese dictionary was stored, and finally by the female students' room. The first of these three is a unique space, with an exposed asymmetrical roof structure and a south wall lined with windows covered by shoji paper. The dictionary is a fascinating document, a testament to the dedication of Japan's early students of European culture.

Returning via Yodoya-bashi to the island and continuing to the west along the Dōjima River (which runs north of the island), the scenery of Nakanoshima takes on a more conventional character, with modern highrise offices, hotels, and elevated expressways dominating the views, though the promenade continues to be an attractive path. When you reach the Osaka University Medical School, turn south to find the last stop on the tour, the Osaka Science Museum.

With this sleek, stylish building, we have completed a journey from the late Edo period through the industrial age and up to the present era. The Science Museum was completed in 1989, and is architecturally an apt representation of the museum's point of view. Its shiny skin of ceramic tile and glass, its combination of curved and rectilinear surfaces, and its vast interior atrium give it a futuristic look. While many of Japan's younger architects express a cynical pessimism toward the state of Japanese society in their work, this building reflects an optimistic, technology-conquers-all vision.

Inside, the latest techniques in computerized graphics, hands-on displays, and electronic theatrics are used throughout to create an atmosphere which is a combination of museum and theme park. Many of the exhibits are informative and entertaining, especially to the young audience at whom they are primarily targeted. English-language materials are relatively sparse; perhaps they were still being developed at the time of my visit.

THE RIVERFRONTS

The most impressive part of the museum is its Science Theater, which doubles as a planetarium and Omnimax film theater. Both are worth seeing; the images are so stunning that it hardly matters whether or not one understands the Japanese narration. The planetarium show offers a city dweller the rare opportunity to see a star-filled sky.

Emerging again into the hazy daylight of the city, there remains only the journey home. Three hundred meters east of the museum is Higo-bashi. Crossing this bridge will bring you to Higobashi Station, the nearest subway stop to the Science Museum. Another half kilometer to the east is Yodoya-bashi Station, from which connections to other subway and train lines may be more convenient.

SEMPU-KAN Interior open only for three days in March, from 10 A.M. to 3:30 P.M. Admission: free.

MINT MUSEUM 9 A.M. to 4 P.M. Monday to Friday; 9 A.M. to 11:30 A.M. the first and third Saturday of every month. Closed Sundays, April 4, and during cherry-blossom season. Admission: free.

FUJITA MUSEUM OF ART Open during scheduled exhibitions only, from 10 A.M. to 4 P.M. Closed Mondays. (tel. 06-351-0582). Admission: ¥1,000.

MUSEUM OF ORIENTAL CERAMICS 9:30 A.M. to 5 P.M. Closed Mondays, the day after national holidays, and from December 28 to January 4. (tel. 06-223-0055). Admission: ¥400.

TEKIJUKU 10 A.M. to 4 P.M. Closed Sundays, Mondays, national holidays, and from December 28 to January 4. Admission: ¥200.

OSAKA SCIENCE MUSEUM 9:30 A.M. to 4:45 P.M. Closed Mondays, the day after national holidays, and from December 28 to January 4. (tel. 06-444-5656). Admission: ¥400, plus ¥600 each for planetarium and Omnimax.

OSAKA BUSINESS PARK

Osaka Business Park (OBP) is a monument to the success of the latest stage in the evolution of Japanese culture, the state-of-the-art electronic consumer society. Created as an entity unto itself, OBP stands in splendid isolation from the old industrial city, rather like the Jetsons' houses in the sky. Each of the corporate towers is likewise designed to stand apart, to impress upon the visitor the wealth, power, and taste of its owner. Inside OBP the world is clean, orderly, and filled with the latest gadgets.

From Kyōbashi Station, on the JR and Keihan lines, an elevated walkway system a few hundred meters long takes you over the Neya River to OBP. A good place to start a visit to the area is at the Twin Towers, which can be entered directly from the walkway.

Twin Towers is the creation of Matsushita Electric, one of Osaka's largest corporations and maker of all manner of electrical and electronic devices under such brand names as National, Panasonic, and Technics. Osaka is Matsushita's home city, and its Twin Towers complex is an expression of its size and status.

There are two showrooms in the National Tower, the northernmost of the pair. On the third floor is the National Living Plaza, which exhibits electrical home furnishings, from can openers to intercoms to air conditioners. Model rooms are furnished with Matsushita's products, displaying the company's idea of the cutting edge in interior design.

Panasonic Square, on the second floor, is a sort of electronic amusement park. You can listen to the latest CDs in audio booths, analyze your golf, tennis, or baseball swing using a stop-motion video setup (which displays it on a giant screen for crowds of onlookers), and play with an array of other gizmos. In spite of its admission charge, Panasonic Square is extremely popular, especially among elementary schoolboys. Most gravitate toward a small cluster of video games, where competition for a chance at playing one is more intense than the games themselves.

There is also an observation deck near the top of the other building of the pair, called the Mid Tower, which features impressive views of the city.

OSAKA BUSINESS PARK

The view from nearby Osaka Castle, however, is roughly equivalent, so the admission charge to the Mid Tower deck might be better spent elsewhere.

Fujitsu and NEC both have buildings in OBP. Their showrooms are considerably more low-key than Panasonic Square, but still contain lots of electronic goodies. Fujitsu Plaza has one room for software and a larger one for hardware (primarily business-oriented), both on the first floor and both free of charge. As at Panasonic Square, the software room is best avoided on weekends and school holidays. The NEC showroom is more traditional; products are abundantly displayed, but there is relatively little hands-on material.

The International Market Place (IMP, to use the inevitable acronym) is a shopping mall featuring imported merchandise. Though pricey fashions predominate, there is an interesting range of goods for sale, from cowboy boots to Italian furniture. My favorite feature of IMP is its Toilets of the World. Each of the six groups of public restrooms contains fixtures imported from a different country, with each room's decor corresponding to the style of the fixture—a sort of national character expressed in plumbing.

Architecturally, the buildings of OBP are typical of high-end corporate styling. For the most part, they have been designed and built by large contractor/architecture/engineering corporations such as Nikken Sekkei and the Osaka-based Takenaka Kōmuten, and are good, crisply detailed representatives of the work of such firms. Among them, the Tokio Marine and Fire Insurance Building, built by the Kajima Corporation, is particularly impressive. Efforts have been made throughout OBP to create pleasant spaces with landscaping, sculpture, and open plazas.

NATIONAL LIVING PLAZA   10 A.M. to 6 P.M. Admission: free.

PANASONIC SQUARE   10 A.M. to 6 P.M. Closed Wednesdays. Admission: ¥400.

MID TOWER OBSERVATION DECK   10 A.M. to 8 P.M. Admission: ¥400.

FUJITSU PLAZA, NEC SHOWROOM, IMP   10 A.M. to 6 P.M. Admission: free.

SHINSAIBASHI

If Osaka has an expatriate center, a rough equivalent to Tokyo's Roppongi, it is Shinsaibashi. Like Roppongi, Shinsaibashi is a gathering place for foreign residents as well as hip young Japanese. The spine of the district is the 600-meter-long Shinsaibashi-suji shopping arcade, reputedly Osaka's busiest. In the arcade, and in the district alongside it, are some of Osaka's priciest boutiques, along with American fast-food chains and even a country-western bar. The arcade is packed night and day, and barely navigable on weekends. Fashionable strollers abound, along with the entire foreign population of the city (or so it seems) and a few homeless people tolerant enough to ignore the cameras and camcorders of tourists in exchange for presumably generous handouts.

Most Japanese shops are open from 10 A.M. until 7 P.M., although some fashionable and youth-oriented stores don't open their doors until noon. A peculiarity of Japanese retailers is that each store sets its own policy concerning which day of the week it will designate as its day off.

Shinsaibashi is also the center for much of Osaka's most exciting modern architecture. Just south of Shinsaibashi Station (map 3), near the north end of the arcade, are two dignified old department stores, the Daimaru, designed in 1932 by William Merrell Vories, and the Sōgō, also from the 1930s, by Murano Tōgō. Although they have been modified both inside and out, the two retain sufficient traces of their original appearance—the view of the facades from Midōsuji and the interior detailing around the elevator lobbies, for example—to make it clear that merchandising was a more decorous business half a century ago.

The arcade is anchored at each end by buildings which express the contemporary approach to marketing with equal eloquence. At the north end is Kurokawa Kishō's Sony Tower, a vertical showroom for the Walkman's inventors. Built in 1976, the tower is a gleaming futuristic monument to the sacred modern notion of endless material progress. The architect has put state-of-the-art construction technology on display, while acknowledging its future obsolescence. Clipped to the side of the building are stainless-steel capsules which hold the building's restrooms. These capsules are symbolically removable, suggesting that changes in plumbing technology will render them outmoded long before the rest of the structure loses its usefulness.

Kurokawa is an Osaka native who now practices in Tokyo. He was one of the proponents of the Metabolist movement in Japanese architecture, a group best known for its sweeping visions of city-sized structures in which the various components—structure, mechanical services, and occupied spaces—are independently expressed and arranged to permit flexibility and change over time. Their visions, conceived in the 1960s, were never realized on a large scale, but buildings like the Sony Tower remain as testament to the optimistic postwar spirit of Japan and the industrialized world.

At the opposite end of the Shinsaibashi-suji arcade is a tower which reveals a darker, more brooding vision of the future. The 1988 Kirin Plaza building was designed by Kyoto-based Takamatsu Shin, perhaps Japan's most prominent young architect. Kirin Plaza is a sharp, cold, and extremely refined exercise in black marble, stainless steel, aluminum, and glass. It is topped by four tall lanterns which turn the building into a giant advertisement at night. The idea of building as billboard has rarely been expressed so blatantly or powerfully. That this is the function of the building is apparent inside; it contains a small bar, restaurant, art gallery, and concert hall, none of them sufficient in size to generate adequate revenue for a building as precious as this. Kirin Plaza is simply a vanity piece for its owner, a highly visible statement of Kirin's corporate taste and wealth. Aesthetically, Takamatsu's buildings show a very different attitude toward Japan's material condition than does Kurokawa's Sony Tower. The glittering materials in the more recent building seem agressive, even threatening, in their insistence on one's attention, while their mechanical perfection discourages human contact.

Two other Kansai district architects of note have buildings in Shinsaibashi. Andō Tadao is an established master, known for his pronounced Osaka dialect and his disdain for traditional architectural training. Andō's buildings are austere, refined structures primarily of bare concrete and glass. Their power is derived from the subtle interplay of geometries and from an almost mystical dialogue between the building and nature, especially in the ever-changing play of light and shade on the bare concrete surfaces. That an architect of such quiet and unmaterialistic buildings is now so often employed by fashion designers is something of a paradox. In fact, his designs are sometimes easy to overlook in the visually competitive environment of Shinsaibashi. On the other hand, his buildings serve as effective backdrops for the dramatic, sensational clothing they contain. Four of Andō's buildings are identified on map 3. My favorite is the Galleria, with its large skylit atrium bounded on one side by a sheer concrete wall and on the other by a complex system of stairs and shop windows. All of Andō's Shinsaibashi buildings act as islands of silence in the crashing sea of commerce surging around them.

Three more of Andō's buildings share a block with another extreme in architectural design. The Children's Museum is the product of a young designer named Wakabayashi Hiroyuki. This building, which is not really a museum but a collection of children's clothing stores, is as loud as Andō's are quiet. It combines a postmodern appropriation of historical motifs—classical columns, broken pediments, and the like—with sloped and curving surfaces covered in irregular, multicolored ceramic tiles, a treatment that echoes the eccentric architecture of Antonio Gaudi. You enter the "museum" via a rocket-shaped elevator, complete with spacesuited attendant, and are launched to the top of the multistoried complex. You make your way back down to street level through a dizzying array of astronomically priced fashions for young children. The building's excessive decoration and screaming exuberance are perhaps as much an ironic comment on the consumer city as an enthusiastic acceptance of it.

Both Andō's and Wakabayashi's buildings are in the section of Shinsaibashi known as Yōroppa Mura (European Village). Invoking the continent of Europe is evidently intended to suggest sophistication and high culture; hence the concentration of international designer boutiques. Across Midōsuji in the western part of Shinsaibashi is Amerika Mura, the upstart companion to Yōroppa.

Those homesick Americans looking for familiar streetscapes will find no solace here. The vision of America found in Amerika Mura seems to have been drawn from a combination of MTV and *Variety* magazine, with a touch of *Cosmopolitan* and *Sports Illustrated* thrown in. Blue jeans, leather jackets, and images of James Dean and Marilyn Monroe are plastered over every available surface in what is otherwise a fairly typical Japanese shopping district. Architecturally, "brash" is certainly the operative word, and examples of every extroverted style are on display, from sixties pop through the latest deconstructivist mode (look for shiny stainless-steel structures slammed at irrational angles into solid walls). Unfortunately, the quality of the designs is generally not strong enough to overcome the atmosphere of disposable culture that pervades the district. If you are looking for live Americans here, your best chance is at the huge Tower Record outlet (actually a misnomer, since they sell only compact disks). It is located two blocks west of Midōsuji, and two and a half blocks north of Dōtombori, at 1-9 Nishi Shinsaibashi. On the whole, the impression of America conveyed by Amerika Mura may make you wish to claim to be Norwegian.

A crowd scene by woodblock artist Yoshiume, dating to the 1850s (courtesy Dean Schwaab).

Left Minoo Falls among the maples in Minoo Quasi-National Park.
Below Pouring water on the moss-covered Mizukake Fudō figures of Hōzen-ji, a temple in Namba.
Right The multiple Jizō figures of Senkō-ji, a temple in Hirano.

Waterfowl habitat in Nankō Wild Bird Sanctuary.

Above The Japanese garden in Expo Park.
Left The atrium of the Galleria shops, designed by Andō Tadao.

Above A medieval streetscape in Tondabayashi City's Jinai-machi.
Below The city as seen from the Tōkai Nature Trail above Minoo Falls.

Above Nakanoshima Central Hall, built in 1908.
Below Osaka Business Park's glittering towers (courtesy Ban PR).

Above The fireworks finale of the Tenjin Festival along Osaka's riverfronts (courtesy Ban PR).
Below Raucous and spirited teamwork during the Tenjin Festival (courtesy Ban PR).

Above A moment of drama and intensity in the Bunraku puppet theater (courtesy National Bunraku Theater).
Below Sakè sets and rice bowls on display at a restaurant supply shop on Dōguya-suji Street.

Above Crowds gathering at the Osaka Aquarium.
Right The fashionable Shinsaibashi shopping arcade at night.
Below right The fourteenth-century image hall of Kanshin-ji, a temple in Kawachi Nagano.

Left Shitennō-ji's urban-density turtle pond.
Above Sumiyoshi Taisha's famous arched bridge.
Right The monumental span of Minato Ōhashi in Osaka Harbor.

Above The National Bunraku Theater, designed by Kurokawa Kishō (courtesy National Bunraku Theater).
Below Azaleas in bloom at Expo Park's Japanese garden.

Left A house perched beside a stream in Fumin no Mori, a prefectural forest.
Below Tosabori River and Nakanoshima Park.

Above The Rokuban Turret of 1628 Osaka Castle.
Below The New Kabuki Theater, designed by Murano Tōgō and built in 1958.

Right Osaka Castle's reconstructed donjon during cherry-blossom season (courtesy Ban PR).
Below The 1907 Nankai Railway Station at Hamadera in Sakai.

Above A map of central Osaka as it existed in 1683 (courtesy Kansai University Library).
Below A woodblock print (c. 1838) of the lighthouse at Sumiyoshi, built in 1796 (courtesy Dean Schwaab).

NAMBA

The Dōtombori Canal separates the Namba district (map 3) from its closely related neighbor, Shinsaibashi. At opposite ends of Ebisu-bashi, the bridge that spans the river at the south end of the Shinsaibashi-suji shopping arcade, two structures signify the differences between the two districts. To the north, Takamatsu Shin's Kirin Plaza is a glittering, self-conscious monument. To the south, the even more renowned giant mechanical crab lurking over the entrance to the Kani Dōraku restaurant (see page 126) appeals more directly and unpretentiously to the consumer masses. Namba is the traditional restaurant, bar, and theater district of Osaka, and retains much of its medieval character, if not its physical remains.

The heart of Namba is the shopping street that parallels the canal and takes its name from it. In the seventeenth century the canal was lined with theaters, as many as twenty at its peak. Fashionable patrons and famous actors made their entrances by boat, and the neighboring restaurants and pleasure houses thrived. The boisterous spirit of that time is captured in a woodblock print by Yoshiume (see photograph following p. 38) that shows crowds of supporters of rival theatrical troupes battling on the street, the theaters with their advertising banners visible in the background. The boat landings are long gone, and the patrons now relatively well-behaved, but several theaters for live performances remain, along with movie theaters. As for pleasure houses, the area between Dōtombori-suji and the National Bunraku Theater now contains a garish cluster of love hotels.

Restaurants dominate the Dōtombori-suji scene today. Osaka's traditional reputation as the city in which to "squander a fortune on food" (my very rough translation of the Japanese *kuidaore*) is easily understood after a few evenings on Dōtombori-suji. The choices are overwhelming and the quality consistently high. Osaka is especially known for its seafood—hence the waving crab, blowfish lanterns, wriggling 30-foot shrimp, and numerous beached fishing boats or fragments and facsimiles thereof to lure the hungry into various eating establishments. The whole of Dōtombori-suji resembles a stage set for a reverse morality play extolling the virtues of gluttony.

Off the main arcade, the streets are narrow and more typical of Japanese dining districts, but the food is equally fine and the atmosphere less frenetic. Particularly reminiscent of the premodern streetscape are the lanes around Hōzen-ji. The temple in its postwar form is quite small, but famed for its Mizukake Fudō statues, moss-covered stone images onto which the faithful splash scoops of water. The combination of the temple roofs and lanterns, the crowds around the statues, and the scent of incense, all in the midst of a lively row of restaurants, makes for an animated and timeless scene.

Oda Sakunosuke, a modern writer of fiction and native of Osaka, well understood the attractions of the district. In a recent translation of his short stories by Burton Watson, the following passage appears—though set in the 1930s, contemporary seekers of gastronomical experience may gain inspiration for their own nocturnal ramblings from the protagonist's approach:

> According to [Ryūkichi], there was nothing good to eat in the north end of Osaka [Umeda]. For really good things you had to go to the southern part of the city. And it was no good going to first class restaurants. It might sound like penny-pinching, but you were just throwing your money away in places like that. . . . They had eel at the Izumiya at the east end of the Aioi Bridge in Dōtombori, octopus at the Takoume in Nipponbashi, *kantō-daki* or vegetables in broth at the Shōbentango-tei in the grounds of Hōzen-ji temple, *tekkamaki sushi* and sea bream skin in vinegar and miso sauce at the Sushisute just in from the Tokiwa Theater in Sennichi-mae . . . one unglamorous dish after another.

At least two of the restaurants named above—Shōbentango-tei and Takoume—are still in business in or near the locations where Oda's character found them. Those two, along with my own choices of restaurants in the Namba area, both "first class" and "unglamorous," are listed in the chapter on dining.

The theaters which gave Dōtombori-suji its original focus now primarily feature what is sometimes called Japanese vaudeville—Rakugo storytelling, comedic forms such as Manzai, and other popular styles. A few blocks south of the canal, however, is the new home of Osaka's greatest contribution to Japanese culture, the National Bunraku Theater.

Bunraku is a uniquely rich and technically complex form of puppet theater, developed around the beginning of the eighteenth century. The Bunraku style of today places the main focus on the intricate puppets and their virtuoso manipulation by as many as three operators working in concert. But the original Bunraku form emphasized the narrator's chanting recitation of the play's text, with music and relatively simple puppetry as accompaniments. This original Bunraku style was developed by the chanter Takemoto Gidayū and the playwright Chikamatsu Monzaemon, and first performed in Osaka at Takemoto's own theater.

The chanting style of storytelling known as Jōruri had its origins centuries earlier in Japan, where itinerant chanters, often Buddhist monks, enjoyed a long popularity. The use of musical accompaniment was likewise a well-established tradition by Gidayū's time. The combination of these elements with puppetry was a more recent innovation, but not the invention of Gidayū . It was rather the combination of Gidayū's genius as a chanter with the exceptional plays written by Chikamatsu that resulted in the flowering of the Bunraku form.

Chikamatsu's plays borrowed from both the major forms of Japanese theater of his time, Noh and Kabuki. The supernatural elements of Noh appealed greatly to the audiences of the time and were perfectly suited to puppets, who could perform feats not achievable by human actors. Kabuki contributed its dramatic gestures and tales of heroism, especially evident in Chikamatsu's historical dramas. But it was the emphasis on the narration that distinguished early Bunraku and that gave Chikamatsu the opportunity to develop his most moving and lasting plays: his domestic dramas.

The domestic dramas (*sewamono*) are plays about people and situations familiar to the middle-class audiences who were the theater's main patrons.

Their plots revolve around the basic conflicts between duty and desire. The pressure to suppress one's feelings when they conflicted with obligations was particularly strong in feudal Japan. Stories such as *The Love Suicides at Sonezaki* (discussed in the chapter on Umeda, page 11, where the tale is set) created the sort of immediate resonance with their audiences that soap operas seem to have today. Chikamatsu's genius as a writer was to transform such material into poetry of the highest order.

The Bunraku puppets resembling those of today were first developed in the 1730s. The increased complexity of the puppets—three operators are required to manipulate their intricate mechanisms—led to plays which depended much more on action and magical transformations of the characters. The continuing popularity of the form led to its influence on Kabuki, which came to emulate the stylized actions of the puppets.

Bunraku today is performed principally at the National Bunraku Theater, home of the national Bunraku company, a magnificent theater opened in 1984 and designed by Kurokawa Kishō. The main theater seats 750, a capacity small enough to ensure good sight lines for all. Acoustics are equally good. Performances are given in six seasons of two weeks each. In contrast to our tradition of puppetry as entertainment for children, Bunraku is very much an adult art form (in fact, our son was the only child in the audience when my family attended one evening). The program is long, but includes a lengthy intermission, during which most patrons eat dinner. In addition, the shows have been designed for contemporary attention spans; plays are often presented in abridged form, and the works are selected to give a representative sampling of styles. A Chikamatsu piece is nearly always on the program, as is at least one which features supernatural transformations. The art of Bunraku is simultaneously alien and universal, fascinating for its technical artifice and emotionally moving in its dramatic impact.

The Bunraku Theater is worth visiting for its architecture alone. Its style represents a departure from Kurokawa's earlier works, such as the Sony Tower in Shinsaibashi. It is neither uncompromisingly modern in form nor coyly postmodern in borrowing motifs from history. Instead, Kurokawa has juxtaposed specific Japanese elements—a curved window high on the facade, for example—with modern geometries and high-tech materials, so that the disparate elements engage in a sort of inconclusive dialogue. This lack of resolution between tradition and modernity is seen in the work of many Japanese architects today, and often results in jarring or brooding compositions. But Kurokawa clearly wants his buildings to be enjoyed as well as pondered, and the questions raised by the juxtaposed forms never impinge too strongly on the beauty and utility of the theater. In fact, they complement the contemporary performance of an anachronistic art form.

Another of Namba's theaters addresses the architectural dialogue between modern and traditional forms. The New Kabuki Theater is no longer new nor used much for Kabuki (it generally features more popular fare, including Broadway-style musicals). The 1958 design by Murano Tōgō is located on Midōsuji just north of the Takashimaya/Nankai complex. The large scale and simple mass of the theater are broken by a series of undulating eaves and capped by a tall gabled roof. This roof is derived from traditional Japanese forms, as are the details of the reinforced concrete structure that supports it. The style of the building is reminiscent of the 1930s, when nationalist sentiments prompted the substitution of Japanese forms for the Greco-Roman elements of classical Western architecture. Murano's design is much more sophisticated than those early attempts at "Japanizing" imported architectural methods. Comfortable working in a variety of styles, the architect selected traditional elements from his repertoire in what must have seemed a natural solution for the design of a Kabuki Theater.

A similar approach was taken by Urabe Shizutarō in his design for the Japan Folk Art Museum, built two years after the New Kabuki Theater on a site a few blocks further south. This building is an abstract version in concrete of a traditional Japanese *kura,* or storehouse. Painted concrete substitutes for mud plaster and bare concrete for tiled roofs. The small windows and the siting of the building in a small fenced-off courtyard are traditional elements that help create a tranquil atmosphere, despite the busy city beyond, in which to enjoy the crafts. The result is a successful fusion of old and new elements into a convincing whole. The interior detailing meshes nicely with the objects on display, managing to be straightforward in function and simple in material yet thoughtfully designed and crafted.

I have singled out these three buildings—the Bunraku Theater, the New Kabuki Theater, and the Japan Folk Art Museum—because they seem to embody the distinctive character of the Namba district: a stubborn insistence upon retaining cultural traditions while avidly pursuing the material benefits of the twentieth century, shrugging off any inherent contradictions in the process. Namba contains more attractions than those I have mentioned here, some discussed elsewhere in this book, others (like the bustling Nankai City Mall and its macho rocket centerpiece) omitted due to simple arbitrariness on my part. Many will insist that Namba is the "real Osaka"—conservative and pragmatic, more involved in the material pleasures and frustrations of daily life than in grand deeds or cosmic speculation. Certainly the visitor to Namba has no excuse to leave without indulging in its worldly enjoyments.

NATIONAL BUNRAKU THEATER Dates vary for the six performance seasons. English programs are available for performances in April, June, July, and August (tel. 06-212-2531). Admission: ¥3,600 to ¥4,300 for adults, half price for students.

JAPAN FOLK ART MUSEUM 10 A.M. to 5 P.M. Closed Mondays. (tel. 06-641-6309). Admission: ¥300.

NEW KABUKI THEATER (tel. 06-631-2121)

SHITENNŌ-JI

Shitennō-ji is Osaka's most ancient and important Buddhist temple. It was founded by Shōtoku Taishi (Prince Shōtoku), Japan's first great patron and promoter of Buddhism, in 593. Only Asuka-dera, a temple in Nara, is older.

Prince Shōtoku was a sort of combination Saint Peter and George Washington, credited as founder of both the religious and civic traditions of the country, though he ruled only as regent, never as emperor. Shōtoku's mytho-history begins with his birth in a stable; he was able to speak as soon as he was born. At age two, he read the Chinese classics and declared his faith in Buddhism. In 592, his aunt, Suiko, became Japan's first historical empress, but Shōtoku ruled beside her as Prince Regent. He was then twenty years old. Though he lived only twenty-nine more years, Shōtoku is credited not only with making Buddhism the state religion but also with establishing central control over the rival clans which had previously resisted the idea of strong imperial authority. He also authored the so-called Seventeen Article Constitution, actually a brief statement of the fundamentals of government (article six, for example, begins, "Punish the wicked and reward the virtuous"). Shōtoku holds an important place in the minds of the Japanese: until recently his face graced both the ¥5,000 and ¥10,000 bills.

Shitennō-ji is dedicated to the Shitennō, or Four Heavenly Kings, who are guardian deities of the four directions. Shōtoku had prayed to these deities for victory in the succession struggle that followed his father's death. The construction of the temple represented both Shōtoku's gratitude at his clan's victory and an appeal for the deities' continued protection of the kingdom.

The location of Shitennō-ji (map 4) is an indication of Osaka's early prominence in the development of Japanese society at the beginning of the historical period. The area was then known as Tsu-no-kuni ("anchorage"), and was the principal port of entry for visitors and goods from overseas. Shitennō-ji was placed at the southern end of a low ridge which overlooked the sandbars and scattered islands of the shallow harbor.

The five-storied pagoda served as a distinctive and impressive landmark for those arriving by sea. Like a modern urban skyline studded with skyscrapers, the complex served to notify visitors of the strength and cultural sophistication of the empire that erected it. The Chinese style of Shitennō-ji's buildings represented the younger and smaller nation's debt to Chinese culture, but also its ambitions to match China's achievements.

Shitennō-ji's original structures have been destroyed and reconstructed numerous times over the course of their fourteen-century history, as a result of both natural and man-made disasters. The most recent reconstruction, in the 1950s, followed damage inflicted during the Second World War. The original ground plan has survived intact, however, and is of considerable significance in the development of Japanese Buddhist architecture.

A rectangular walled compound surrounds the three principal buildings of the original temple. It is entered through the Chūmon, or Middle Gate, which faces south, the most auspicious compass direction. Minor entrances also occur on the east and west walls, but the north edge is unbroken, protecting against the evil influences which might enter from that direction. Arranged symmetrically along the north-south axis are the pagoda, the Kondō (Golden Hall), and the Kōdō (Lecture Hall). The strict symmetry of the layout is most probably a direct copy of a continental (Chinese or Korean) prototype, and is the only surviving example of the type in Japan.

Unfortunately, the buildings in the original compound have been reconstructed not in wood but in reinforced concrete. The resulting structures, though thoroughly researched to follow the original Asuka-period style, appear heavy and artificial. The aesthetic appeal of wooden architecture has as much to do with its tactile appeal up close as with its overall geometry. The uniqueness of the grain and weathering patterns in each piece of wood and the subtlety with which wooden elements can be carved and fitted are not reproducible in concrete. As a result the buildings are impressive from a distance but disappointing at close range.

Shitennō-ji has continued to grow throughout its long history, with new structures reflecting the development of Japanese Buddhism and society. Due west of the original temple's west gate is a stone torii, constructed in

1294. The torii is a Shinto form, and its presence at Shitennō-ji indicates the blending of the two faiths in Japan.

The torii is related to a ritual called *nissō-kan*, a meditation on the setting sun, which was practised at Shitennō-ji. Understanding the beauty and impact of the ceremony today, as taxis and trucks belching noxious fumes rumble just outside the gate, requires a leap of the imagination. You must simply accept that the view from Uemachi Ridge to the west, overlooking Osaka Bay in the days before industrial urbanization and land reclamation, was a spectacular one, spectacular enough to draw pilgrims from throughout Japan to Shitennō-ji's *nissō-kan*.

The paradise of Amida Buddha was considered to be in the west, and the torii was located so that on the spring and autumn equinoxes the light of the setting sun would shine through it and directly into the main temple compound through its west gate. An inscription on the torii describes it as the "eastern gate of the Western Paradise," suggesting both the importance of Shitennō-ji and the quality of the view. The selection of a Shinto form for the gate may stem from the fact that the sun—in the guise of the goddess Amaterasu—is the principal deity of Shinto and the progenitor of the imperial family and, hence, the source of the Japanese nation.

Other buildings at Shitennō-ji have survived from the Edo period, the time of Osaka's ascendancy as an economic power. The Rokuji-dō, located due north of the original compound, is an impressive image hall constructed in 1623. In front of the hall is a platform on which Bugaku is performed. Bugaku is a Chinese court dance brought to Japan in the seventh century, and performed in an unbroken tradition through to the present day at only a few sites in Japan. Flanking the platform are ponds which are home to a group of turtles whose population density approaches that of the subways at rush hour.

Gochikō-in is a sub-temple located in the northeast corner of the Shitennō-ji compound. Like the Rokuji-dō, it was built early in the seventeenth century. Gochikō-in is a tranquil enclave within the temple complex, being the most removed from the modern city that surrounds it.

SHITENNŌ-JI

Shitennō-ji's treasure hall is a modern concrete building similar in form to a traditional Japanese storehouse. The works within are extraordinary. Some fragments of textile and a sword are said to have been the property of Prince Shōtoku himself; they are at least roughly contemporaneous with him. The sculpture collection includes a small bronze from the same period, and many fine later pieces. Paraphernalia related to the Bugaku include masks and drums. Most famous of all are the Heian-period (794–1185) fans with sutras written in exquisite calligraphy, accompanied by painted scenes of everyday life.

SHITENNŌ-JI Main compound open from 8 A.M. to 4:30 P.M. from April 1 to September 30; 8:30 A.M. TO 4 P.M. from October 1 to March 31. Closed Mondays. Admission: ¥200 (includes admission to the treasure hall).

BUGAKU AT SHITENNŌ-JI Dances are performed three times a year, on February 15, April 22, and September 8.

UEMACHI RIDGE

Along the west side of the Uemachi Ridge, between Tennō-ji Park and the Tanimachi 9-chōme subway station, lies an area that retains some of the flavor of medieval Osaka. A combination of factors has led to its partial preservation. Numerous small temples and shrines have kept land out of the hands of developers; the steep western slope of the ridge has been a disincentive to development; and a number of structures, through sheer luck, managed to survive the Second World War. A walk in this neighborhood conveys a sense of the geography of Uemachi Ridge, the principal topographic feature in the otherwise flat terrain of Osaka. It also leads past several interesting old temples and shrines, and along attractive stone-paved slopes. The route shown on map 4 follows, for the most part, a historical walk designated by the city of Osaka, and identifiable by a pattern of brick and pebbles set into the pavement. The grounds of most temples and shrines are always open to the public, and there is usually no admission charged.

Leaving Shitennō-ji by the west gate, a short walk to the west brings you to Isshin-ji. This temple is among the most popular in Osaka, especially as a site for memorial services for the dead and as a repository for their ashes. The Nokotsu-dō contains a Buddha image which is actually made from cremated human remains sent to Isshin-ji from throughout Japan. The statue is remade using newly donated remains approximately every ten years in a tradition dating back to the mid-nineteenth century. (The Buddha image which is replaced is presumably given a suitable burial.)

Almost completely destroyed in the Second World War, the reconstructed traditional buildings are unspectacular. There is, however, an interesting modern building designed in 1977 by Takaguchi Yasuyuki, who is both an architect and the head priest of the temple. The structure combines concrete, a steel space frame, and a tiled roof in a unique blending of traditional and modern forms.

From Isshin-ji, the walking course crosses Highway 25 and proceeds north through a small shrine, Yasui Jinja. Then turn east up Tenjin-zaka, the first of the several old pedestrian streets along the west slope of the ridge. Turning north again, you soon reach Kiyomizu-dera. This temple was named after the famous Kyoto temple which is similarly, if more dramatically, perched on the edge of a steep hillside from which a spring of clear water (*kiyomizu*) issues. Osaka's Kiyomizu-dera is modest, but the area around the spring is an attractive grotto. The spring was well known in the Edo period as a source of pure drinking water, prized especially by local intellectuals and other connoisseurs of tea.

North of the temple are two pleasant walking slopes, Kiyomizu-zaka and Aizen-zaka, which lead to the temple Shōman-in, also called Aizen-dō. The Aizen-dō is a *tahōtō*-style pagoda for which the temple is famous. The tahōtō form combines the Indian burial mound shape, called the stupa, with the more common pagoda type derived from Chinese towers. Aizen-dō is thought to have been built in 1594 under the patronage of Toyotomi Hideyoshi. It is among Osaka's oldest surviving buildings and is a beautiful example of the relatively rare tahōtō style. Standing in front of the pagoda is the image hall, built in 1618 under the patronage of the Tokugawa clan. The image hall is a rather stodgy companion to the pagoda; the relationship of the buildings is suggestive of the contrast between the flamboyant Hideyoshi and the more legalistic Tokugawa.

The remainder of the walk north to Tanimachi 9-chōme includes three more pedestrian slopes. One of these, Gakuen-zaka, has been converted into a modern road. The other two, Kuchinawa-zaka and Genshōji-zaka, retain their stone paving and an atmosphere of serenity. (The name Kuchinawa-zaka is said to derive from the local dialect's word for "snake," referring to the undulating rise and fall of the path.) The stretch of road north from Gakuen-zaka to the Ikutama Jinja, a Shinto shrine, makes a transition from a quiet neighborhood of small Buddhist temples to a neon-and-glitz row of love hotels, marking the end of the historical stroll with a loud blast of contemporary culture.

TENNŌ-JI

The district around Tennō-ji Park is the southernmost of the transportation hubs scattered throughout the city of Osaka. Its prominence is due to the convergence of six rail lines: two subway lines, the JR loop line, the Nankai and Kintetsu lines, and the quaint Hankai streetcar line. In character, Tennō-ji is generally less glitzy than Namba and Umeda; it's a center for the plain folks. The area seems less affected by the sweeping postmodernization of the last few decades than do Osaka's other major centers.

At the southeast corner of the intersection formed by the several Tennō-ji stations is the main entrance to Tennō-ji Park, a large and varied urban park, established in the first decade of this century and undergoing a renaissance of sorts. The park was established in 1909, and was expanded over several stages in succeeding decades. Its zoo opened in 1915; a Japanese garden owned by the Sumitomo family on adjacent land was donated in 1921; and the Osaka Municipal Museum of Art was completed on the grounds in 1936.

A more recent project has been the subject of local controversy. Until 1987, the park had been open to the public free of charge. It became known as a refuge for Osaka's homeless population, and its condition became increasingly unsightly. In connection with an exposition held in 1987, the main plaza of the park was renovated, entrance gates added, and an admission charge was introduced. Protesters argued that forcing the homeless from the park for the sake of cleaning up its image was inhumane, but the project went ahead.

The results were clearly an aesthetic success, however one judges the social costs. The plaza is a delightful space of flowers, greenery, sculpture, and fountains, crowned by a fascinating, quirky building designed by Andō Tadao, Osaka's world-renowned architect. The building's peculiarity is the result of a unique combination of functions. Half of the building consists of a large greenhouse in the form of a cubic concrete skeleton filled with glass and topped by a translucent pyramid. The remainder of the structure is a low, windowless cylinder of unadorned concrete, housing a super-wide-screen cinema. The combination of bright and dark spaces, open and closed forms, in a single structure has been admirably expressed by Andō in what is his first public building in Osaka.

The Tennō-ji Zoo is among Japan's oldest, and like many older urban zoos the world over, it generally seems a cramped and unhappy home for its inmates. Recent projects have improved some sections of the zoo, most spectacularly in the addition of a large free-flight bird cage. The cuddly, crowd-pleasing koalas have been given a new home worthy of their star status.

The Municipal Museum of Art dates from 1936. In spite of a 1979 renovation, the building still seems a tired and unlovable container for its superb collection. The collection includes many of the most important artifacts of temples all over the prefecture, on permanent loan to the museum—presumably in order to better safeguard and conserve them. (The treasure halls of some Osaka temples display only facsimiles of their finest pieces; the originals are in the galleries or storerooms of the Municipal Museum of Art.)

The best-known part of the museum's collection is a large group of Chinese paintings known as the Abe Collection in honor of the individual who donated them. The paintings range from the ninth century through the Ch'ing dynasty (1644–1912), and include many superb examples.

Keitaku-en, the Japanese garden in Tennō-ji park, is a pleasant if not inspired stroll garden in the style favored by Edo-period daimyo. In this case, the patron was a plutocrat of the Sumitomo family, who had the garden built for his private use in 1908, donating it to the city some thirteen years later. In a manner reminiscent of the Tribune Tower in Chicago, which is studded with architectural fragments from around the world collected by *Chicago Tribune* newspaper reporters, Keitaku-en contains famous stones and trees obtained from gardens throughout Japan.

At the west edge of Tennō-ji Park is the Shin-Sekai gate, beyond which lies an entertainment district that seems to embody the common, and sometimes downright seedy, character of the area around Tennō-ji Station. The area known as Shin-Sekai (literally "new world") is promoted as a casual, inexpensive restaurant and nightlife district, but is said, by more candid locals, to be the favorite hangout for Osaka's sizable yakuza (gangster) population. There has been some revival in the popularity of the district in recent years; fashionable youth have returned in significant numbers, perhaps due to the overcrowding of their Shinsaibashi and Namba hangouts to the north, perhaps because of the macho value attached to seeking out the city's cheapest fugu, or blowfish, which is poisonous if not skillfully prepared.

Shin-Sekai's symbol is the Tsūtenkaku, a steel tower about 103 meters tall. Like many of Osaka's monuments, Tsūtenkaku has had a difficult history. When originally constructed in 1912, it was both the tallest man-made structure in Asia and the first to feature a passenger elevator. It was partially destroyed during the Second World War, though not, as one might expect, by American bombs. The Japanese Imperial Army was running short of steel in 1943, and dismantled the upper sections of the tower to salvage this strategic material. Reconstructed in 1956, the current Tsūtenkaku can claim no superlatives. It is still a dominant landmark of the southern end of the city, and the view from its observation deck is a fine one. Tsūtenkaku stands as a typical representative of the tower-making compulsion that gripped major cities throughout Japan in the period of modernization, an unfortunate manifestation of the potency and appeal of Paris's Eiffel Tower.

A subsection of Shin-Sekai called Jan-Jan Yokochō specializes in low-cost dining; its name derives from the sound of *shamisen* music which wafted from houses of pleasure during the Edo period, when this was Osaka's licensed red-light district. The clubs and strip shows still in evidence in Shin-Sekai today provide a sort of historical continuity, though one which contemporary promoters might not welcome. Jan-Jan Yokochō is a north-south lane running along the eastern edge of Shin-Sekai, south of the park's Shin-Sekai gate. Following the lane to its southern end will bring you to the tracks of the JR loop line and, below them, the entrance to the Dōbutsuen-mae subway station.

TENNŌ-JI

TENNŌ-JI PARK 9:30 A.M. to 5 P.M. (to 9 P.M. from July 1 to August 31). Closed Mondays. Admission: ¥150.

TENNŌ-JI ZOO 9:30 A.M. to 5 P.M. Admission: ¥400.

OSAKA MUNICIPAL MUSEUM OF ART 9:30 A.M. to 5 P.M. (to 9 P.M. from July 1 to August 31). Closed Mondays. (tel. 06-771-4874). Admission: ¥150.

TSŪTENKAKU 10:30 A.M. to 6:30 P.M. (to 9 P.M. from July 1 to August 31). Closed Sundays and holidays. Admission: ¥500.

MAPS

UMEDA

1. Hankyu tracks
2. Sanbangai North
3. Sanbangai South (Hankyu Umeda Station above)
4. Midōsuji Line Umeda Station
5. Osaka Station
6. Hankyu department store
7. Puchishan Mall
8. Whity Central
9. Whity North 1
10. Whity North 2
11. Whity East
12. Whity South
13. Hanshin Mall
14. ACTY Osaka
15. Central Post Office
16. Hanshin Hotel
17. Hanshin Line Umeda Station
18. Hanshin department store
19. Yotsubashi Line Nishi Umeda Station
20. Dōjima Mall
21. Osaka Ekimae buildings
22. Tanimachi Line Higashi Umeda Station
23. Shin Hankyu Building
24. Ohatsu-tenjin-dōri
25. Oimatsu-dōri (Garou-dōri)

RESTAURANTS

26. Isaribi
27. Ichiriki
28. Hideyoshi
29. Honjin

HOTELS

30. Umeda OS Hotel
31. Osaka Hilton
32. Osaka Terminal Hotel

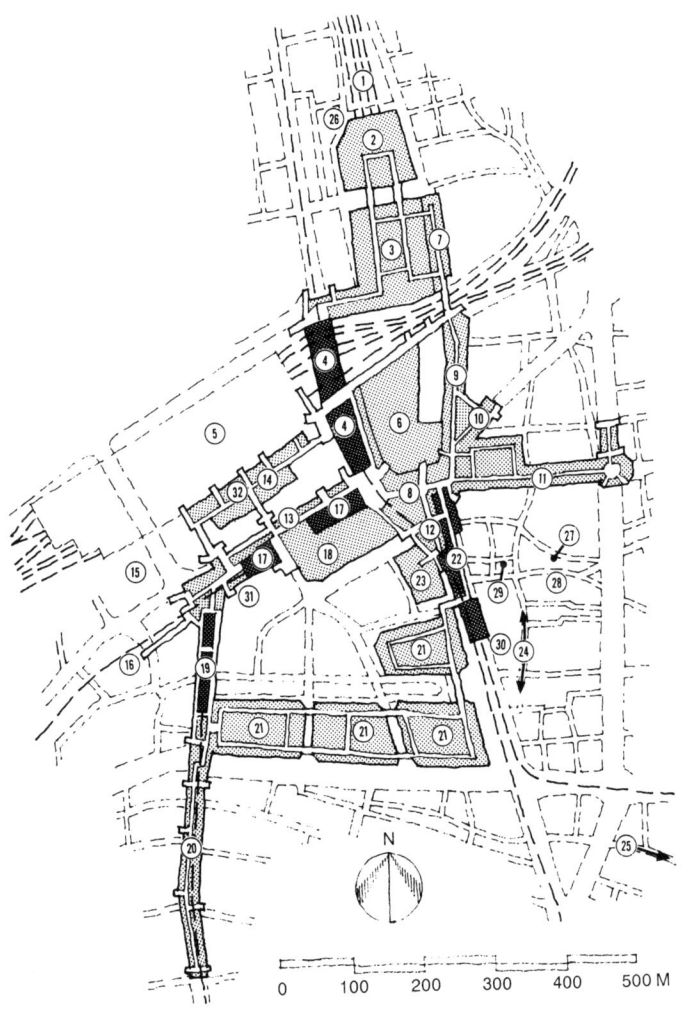

THE RIVERFRONTS

1. Sakuranomiya Station, JR loop line
2. Sakuranomiya Park
3. Yodo River
4. Sakuranomiya-bashi
5. Sempu-kan and Mint portal
6. Osaka Mint; Mint Museum
7. Kawasaki-bashi
8. Fujita Museum of Art
9. Tenjin-bashi
10. Nakanoshima Kōen
11. Naniwa-bashi
12. Museum of Oriental Ceramics
13. Nakanoshima Central Hall
14. Osaka Prefectural Library
15. Osaka City Hall
16. Suishō-bashi
17. Bank of Japan
18. Yodoya-bashi
19. Tekijuku
20. Dōjima River
21. Osaka Science Museum
22. Higo-bashi
23. Higobashi Station

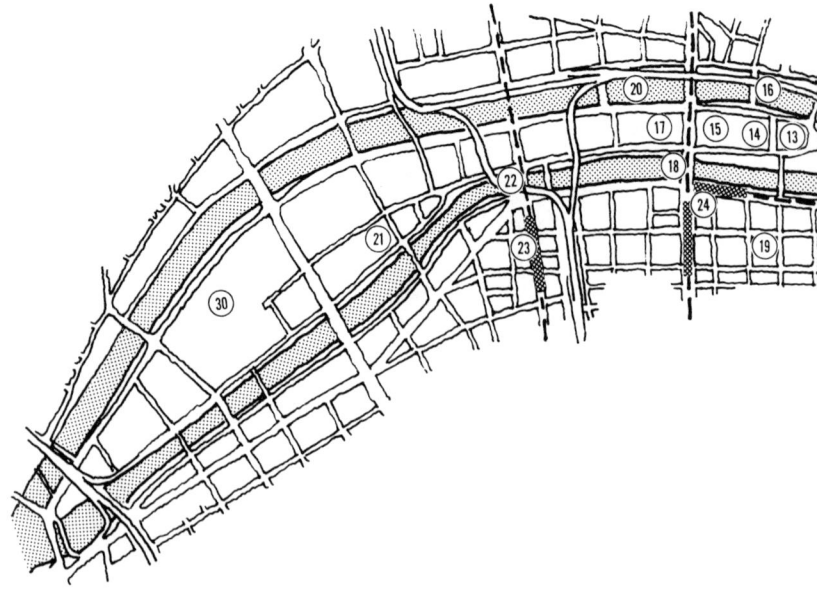

24. Yodoyabashi Station
25. Kitahama Station
26. Temmabashi Station

RESTAURANTS

27. Country Life
28. Taikō-en

HOTELS

29. Osaka Castle Hotel
30. Royal Hotel

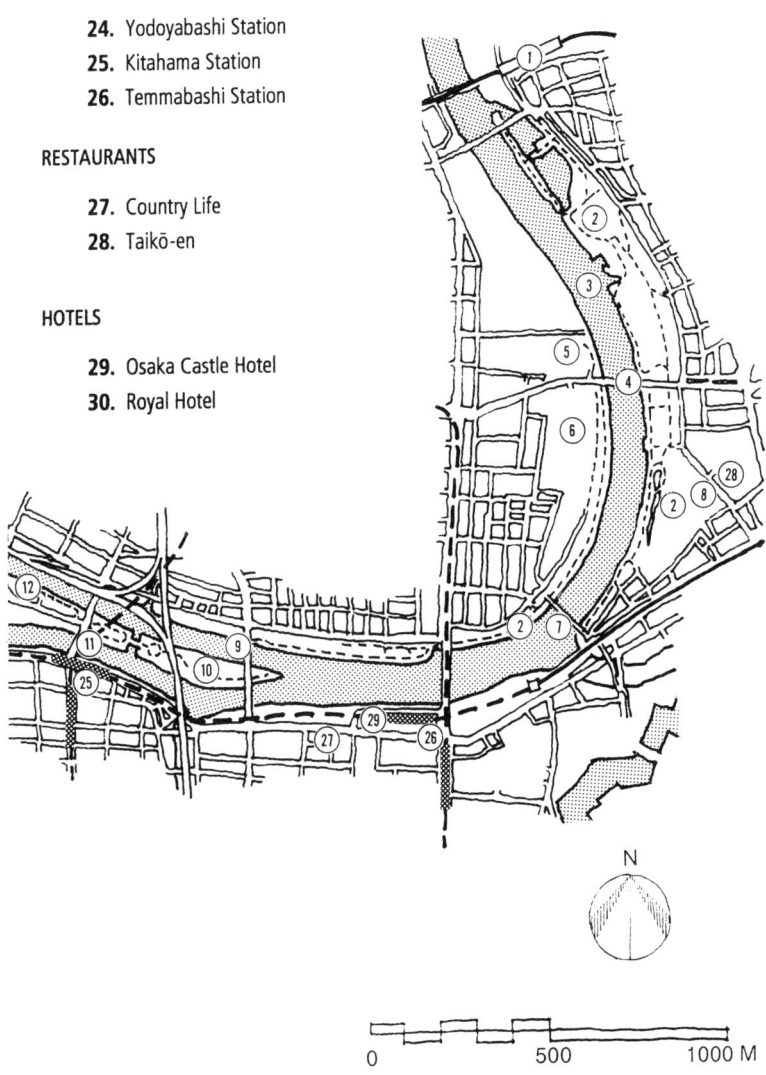

SHINSAIBASHI AND NAMBA

1. Shinsaibashi Station
2. Sogo department store
3. Daimaru department store
4. Shinsaibashi-suji shopping arcade
5. Sony Tower
6. Kirin Plaza
7. Galleria
8. Three buildings by Andō Tadao; Children's Museum
9. Yoroppa Mura
10. Amerika Mura
11. Dōtombori Canal
12. Dōtombori-suji
13. Hōzen-ji
14. National Bunraku Theater
15. Nipponbashi stations
16. Namba subway station, Midōsuji Line
17. Namba stations, Chūō subway and Kintetsu lines
18. New Kabuki Theater
19. Japan Folk Art Museum
20. Takashimaya/Nankai Complex
21. Dōguya-suji

RESTAURANTS

22. Nishike
23. Shirukiyo
24. Pig and Whistle
25. Maruman Honke
26. Kani Doraku; Moti
27. Shobentango-tei
28. Sumo Chaya
29. Aji-bil
30. Takoume

HOTELS

31. Hotel Nikko Osaka
32. Holiday Inn Nankai-Osaka
33. Capsule Hotel Asahi Plaza Shinsaibashi
34. Business Hotel Ohtani
35. Imperial Hotel (Teikoku Hoteru)
36. D-Hotel

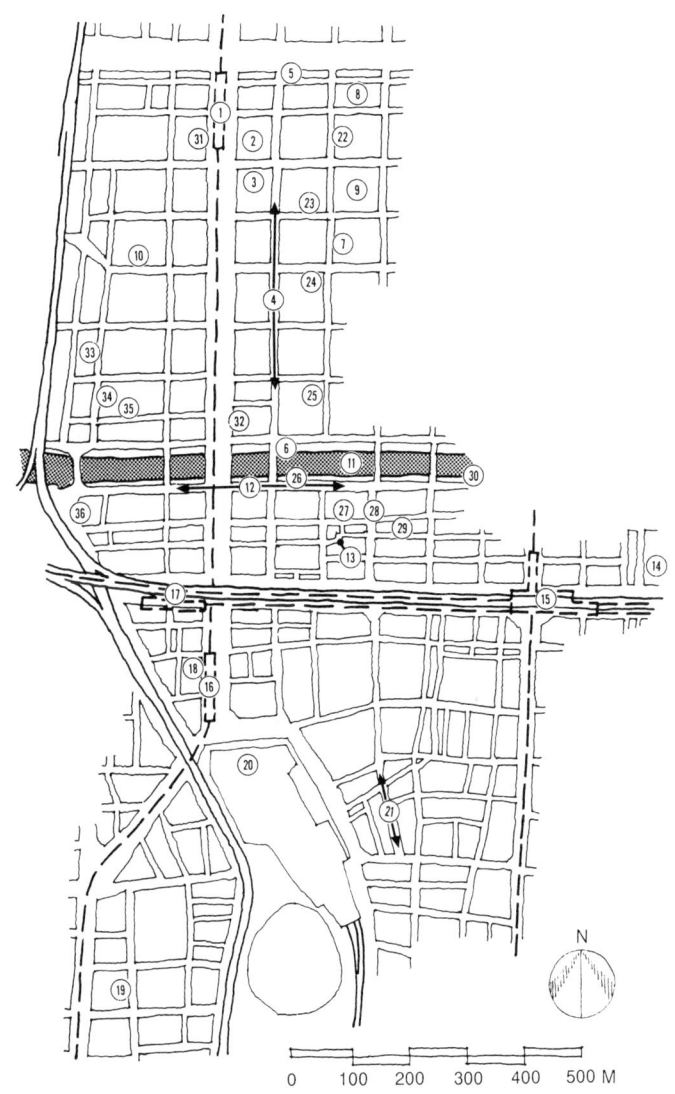

SHITENNŌ-JI AND UEMACHI RIDGE

1. Shitennōji-mae Station
2. Shitennō-ji, original compound
3. Stone torii
4. Rokuji-do
5. Gochiko-in
6. Isshin-ji
7. Tenjin-zaka
8. Kiyomizu-dera
9. Kiyomizu-zaka
10. Aizen-zaka
11. Shoman-in
12. Kuchinawa-zaka
13. Gakuen-zaka
14. Genshōji-zaka
15. Ikutama Jinja
16. Tanimachi 9-chōme Station
17. Kintetsu Uehonmachi Station

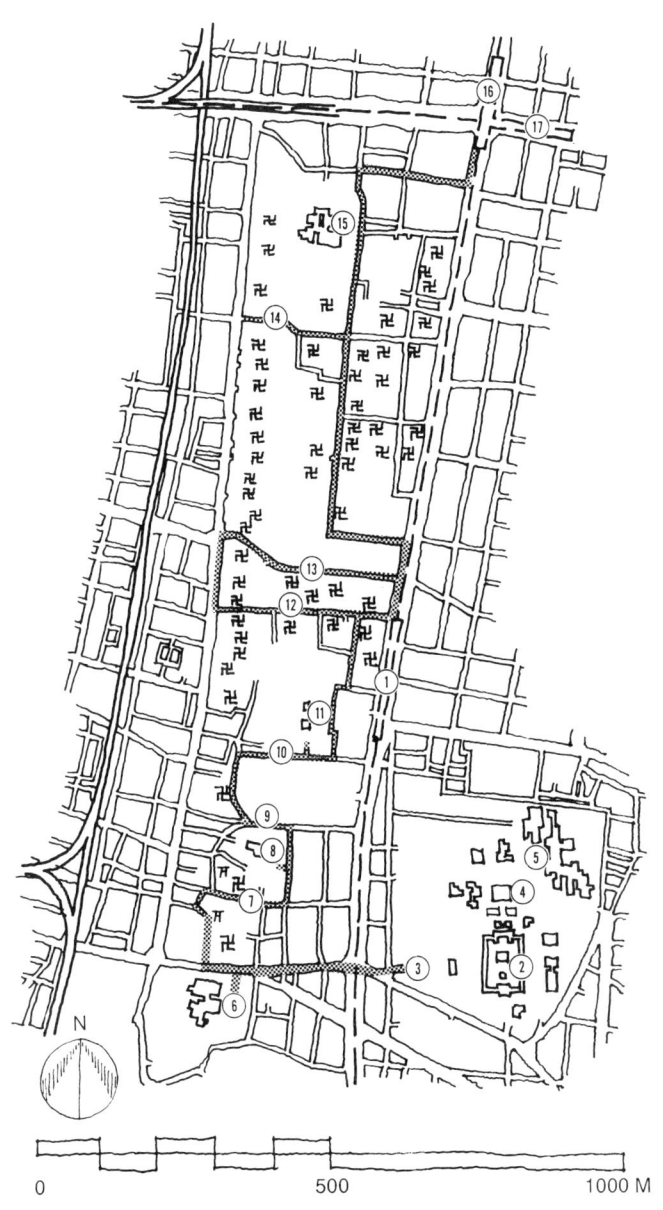

HIRANO

1. Hirano Station
2. Dainembutsu-ji
3. Kumata Jinja
4. Senkō-ji
5. Sanjubu Jinja
6. Hirano Kōen
7. Okuda House
8. JR Kami Station

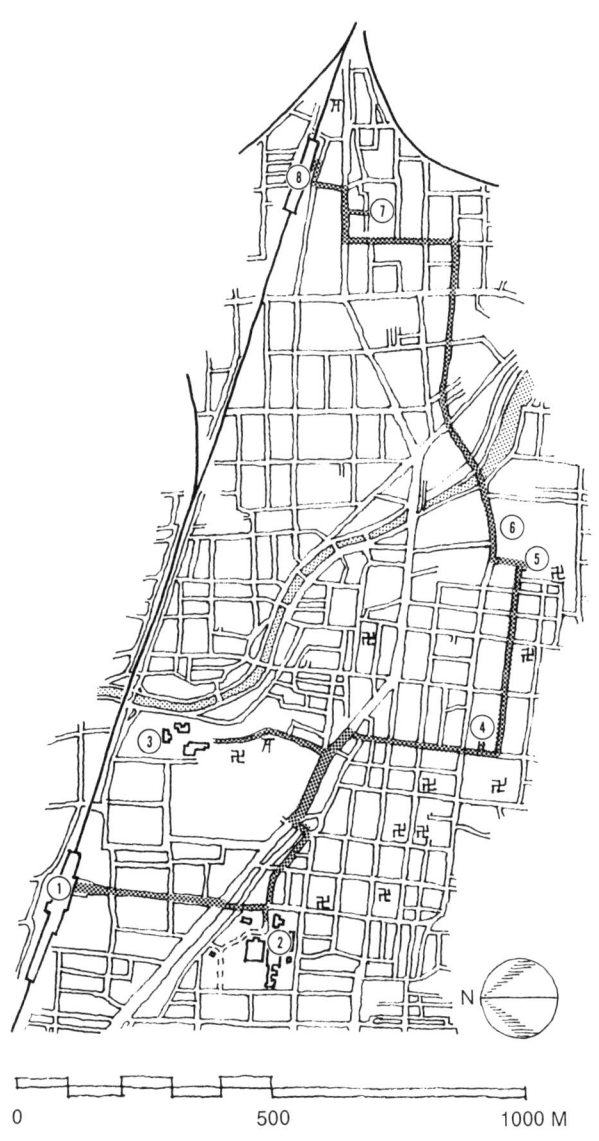

TONDABAYASHI CITY

1. Tondabayashi Station
2. Sugiyama Residence; Jinai-machi Museum
3. Tondabayashi Nishiguchi Station
4. Kawanishi Station
5. Nishikiori Jinja
6. Peace Tower
- Tokugawa-period or Meiji-era machiya

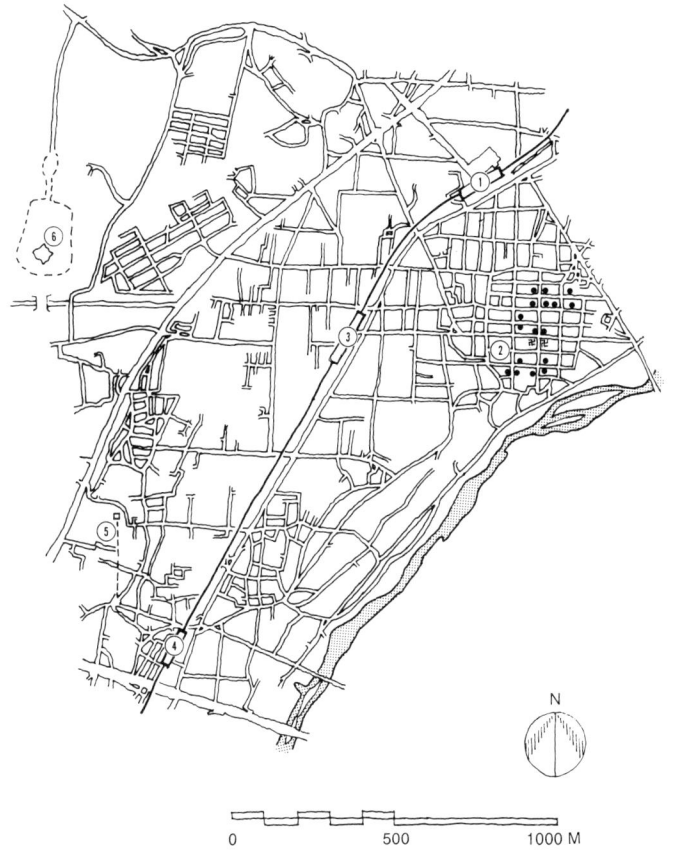

OUTSIDE THE LOOP

SUMIYOSHI

The oldest of the great historic sites within the city of Osaka is Sumiyoshi Taisha, a Shinto shrine. Well south of the JR loop, the Sumiyoshi district is a relatively low-key residential area. With the great shrine as its nucleus, a visit to the district is one of the most pleasant duties of one who seeks old Osaka.

Sumiyoshi can be reached either from Namba, on the Nankai Line, or from Tennō-ji, via the Hankai streetcar. The latter is an enjoyably anachronistic ride, the last of its kind in Osaka. The Hankai Tennō-ji Station is located, oddly, in the middle of the street immediately west of the Kintetsu department store. The tracks follow the street for several blocks, then veer off on their own right-of-way, finally rejoining the street before ending at Sumiyoshi Kōen Station. The Nankai Line, a modern elevated train, stops at Sumiyoshi Taisha Station, immediately adjacent to (and above) the Sumiyoshi Kōen Station.

Before visiting the shrine, it is best to get oriented by heading west from the station, into and through Sumiyoshi Kōen. Across the street from the western entrance to the park stands a stone lighthouse, now incongruously landlocked. It is Japan's oldest lighthouse, dating from the eighteenth century, and was originally located about a hundred meters further west. Today even that location is several kilometers inland, but its presence here serves as a reminder of the dramatic alterations of the coastline made in this century. A series of woodblock prints illustrating famous places in the Osaka area shows the lighthouse as it appeared in 1796 (see last page of photographs, bottom).

Heading back into the park, you'll see a stone relief carving showing a fanciful view of the relationship between sea, lighthouse, and shrine, spatially compressed but conceptually accurate, for the harbor is the origin of Sumiyoshi Taisha. As you head east through the park toward the main entrance to the shrine, try to imagine that the tall pines and spreading camphor trees of the park stand on a beach of white sand, that the odors of the city are replaced by the tang of salt air, and that the view behind you is of ever-changing sandbars, born and swept away at the whim of tide, wind, and waves. This is the true setting of Sumiyoshi Taisha.

SUMIYOSHI

The shoreline region near Sumiyoshi was traditionally called Suma, and was a famous if melancholy setting for several works of Japanese literature. The first to immortalize Suma in verse was the ninth-century courtier Ariwara no Yukihira, who was briefly exiled there. His poem appears in the *Kokinshū* and is given here in my paraphrase of Miyeko Murase's translation:

> Should anyone inquire after me,
> Tell him I am on the beach at Suma,
> Making salt from seawater.

Both the fact of Ariwara's exile there and the mood of the poem indicate that this was an isolated, rather barren region. The theme of exile at Suma was next used by Murasaki Shikibu in her classic eleventh-century novel, the *Tale of Genji*. Prince Genji voluntarily accepts a temporary exile at Suma in order to escape his troubles in the Kyoto court. Although Genji frequently refers to the site as "desolate," his observations are more indicative of his emotional state than of the landscape. In an unusually upbeat passage, Genji sketches the coastline, to the delight of his retainers, then reflects that the beauty of the scene—the sunset and fishing boats on the water—is ample consolation for his troubles.

Still later, Suma became the setting for one of Japan's most famous Noh plays, *Matsukaze*, written in the fifteenth century by Seami Motokiyo. In the play, which imagines the courtier Ariwara no Yukihira's involvement with two Suma maidens named Matsukaze and Murasame during his exile, a solitary pine tree on the beach represents the melancholy of the remote shoreline.

The founding of Sumiyoshi Taisha itself figures in another famous semi-historical tale. According to traditional lore, the Empress Jingū established the shrine in gratitude to the gods of the sea for their protection following a successful excursion to Korea. Jingū became empress following the death of her husband, the Emperor Chūai. Although pregnant at the time, she immediately undertook to fulfill a mission given her by the gods (but disapproved of by her late husband) to invade and conquer Korea. After setting sail from Osaka, her fleet was caught in a storm. Jingū's pleas to the gods of the sea were heeded, and a group of large fishes carried the ships safely to their destination. Under the circumstances, the king of Korea found it prudent to submit to the empress, who then returned in triumph, laden with booty, and soon afterward gave birth to the future Emperor Ōjin. Sumiyoshi Taisha was dedicated shortly thereafter, and has from that day hence been a shrine especially revered by sailors and fishermen. Traditional dating places this event in A.D. 200, but modern scholars believe it occurred in the fourth or early fifth century.

The shrine itself is a large and impressive compound, befitting its status as one of Japan's Grand Shrines (Taisha means "Grand Shrine," the second most important category of Shinto shrine). Its buildings and grounds were spared during the Second World War, and an atmosphere of antiquity pervades the precincts. Stone lanterns donated by patrons of the shrine in hopes of receiving blessings similar in kind, if not in proportion, to those granted the empress line the entrance paths, shaded by magnificent old trees—themselves subjects of reverence in the animistic cosmos of Shinto. The arched bridge over a pond which leads into the inner compound is among Sumiyoshi's most famous and picturesque sites. The original bridge is said to have been built in the time of Hideyoshi at the end of the sixteenth century, during Osaka's great flourishing, and the modern reconstruction certainly conveys the robust confidence of Hideyoshi's time.

Within the inner compound are the four main buildings, all designated as National Treasures. Like all of Japan's ancient shrines the structures have been repeatedly rebuilt over the centuries, each time with the intention of restoring the buildings to their original form. In the case of Sumiyoshi Taisha, the most recent reconstruction occurred in 1810. Each building consists of two parts, an entrance "porch" and an inner sanctuary, the interior of which is completely concealed from view. It is this inner sanctum that is believed to house the deity, and that is also thought to represent the original, fourth-century style of architecture. (The porches, with their curved multiple gables and elaborate details, are in the style of the late sixteenth century, probably designed contemporaneously with the arched bridge.) The inner buildings at Sumiyoshi have distinct characteristics which represent the most sophisticated of the styles found among the Grand Shrines. The

SUMIYOSHI

"Sumiyoshi style" is thought to represent a third step in the evolution of Shinto architecture, beyond the most primitive type seen at Izumo (in western Honshu) and the more symmetrical form found at Ōtori (also in Osaka Prefecture, and discussed in my chapter on Sakai, page 82). The style is distinguished by its increased depth, from two to four bays, which permitted the interior to be subdivided into two separate sanctuaries. The Sumiyoshi buildings are also the oldest of the Grand Shrines to have been traditionally painted in the brilliant red associated with Chinese and Korean architecture; perhaps Empress Jingū's Korean adventure influenced the choice of paint rather than the usual unfinished wood.

Continuing east out of the inner compound you'll find a group of lesser structures worth exploring. The storehouses are massive, unpainted, and wooden, their stout appearance well suited to their function. Several ancient trees are draped in ropes, marking them as sacred; the small shrines in front of them are popular, and incense smoke rises continuously to mingle with the leaves and branches.

Near the south end of the shrine precincts is a rice paddy, the focus of Sumiyoshi's most popular annual festival. Otaue-Shinji, the ceremonial rice planting, is said to have originated with none other than Empress Jingū, who visited the shrine one spring to ask the gods for a plentiful rice harvest. Bringing with her retinue a group of women farmers from what is now Yamaguchi Prefecture, she established a small rice paddy on the grounds of the shrine. The custom of having the emperor plant rice as a ceremonial request for a good harvest continues. Although the Sumiyoshi Shrine is not the site of the imperial ceremony today, the festival here is a lively and elaborate one, involving both adults and children dressed in the ancient costumes of courtiers, dancers, and warriors. The centerpiece of the festival, the rice planting itself, is both a solemn and a comical event. The bull that plows up the paddy is an impressive animal, ceremonially dressed and led by white-clad priests; but often the animal is clearly not accustomed to working the fields, and seems reluctant and a bit confused when brought into the flooded paddy and harnessed to the antique wooden plow. The rice planters, divided into segregated teams of men and women (the idea of relying only on women planters was perhaps too much for the patriarchy to bear at some point in the festival's history), accomplish their task with considerably more competence than the bull. The anachronistic eyeglasses and Rolex watches on the traditionally garbed farmers give the ritual an appropriately modern touch. The festival is held on June 14.

The shrine is host to several other festivals, and is an especially popular destination for the traditional New Year's Eve shrine visit, since its status as Osaka's most important shrine makes it the most auspicious choice. Once every sixty days is a "Dragon Day" according to the traditional calendar. On each Dragon Day, a flea market is held at the shrine, with a wide range of merchandise available, as well as food stands and perhaps even an itinerant fortuneteller.

Resuming our tour of the shrine precincts, one more monument is deserving of a visit. Ōama Jinja, a shrine located at the north end of the grounds, has the distinction of being the oldest building remaining at Sumiyoshi. Constructed in 1708, it has the patina of age which you may have found lacking in the central buildings, though it cannot match their monumental presence.

The north gate of Sumiyoshi Taisha is adjacent to the Ōama Jinja, and if you continue due north on the street opposite this gate, a short walk brings you to another fine old shrine, the Ikune Jinja. Built in 1600, the architectural style reveals the opulence and love of display characteristic of the Momoyama period (1568–1615) and its flamboyant leader, Toyotomi Hideyoshi. While elements of the style are clearly visible in the Sumiyoshi porches, their expression was restrained by the venerable sanctuaries to which they were attached. At Ikune, the style was given free rein, from the copper-roofed and elegantly detailed porch to the inner sanctum, with its multiple gables jauntily projecting toward the sky. Intimate, almost miniature in scale, this shrine is a real delight.

It is also the final stop on my Sumiyoshi tour. Retracing your steps to the Taisha's north gate, you can turn west and quickly reach the streetcar's Sumiyoshi Station, or continue back through the shrine grounds to the west entrance and the Nankai Station.

HIRANO

Southeast of Tennō-ji Station is a district called Hirano. Hirano has an ancient history, dating back to the fifth century A.D., when Korean immigrants were housed here. No artifacts remain from this earliest recorded settlement, and the small ninth-century burial mound, the oldest remaining monument, is of interest only to the most dedicated history buffs. The town later developed as a farming community containing several temples and shrines and a small business district. Today Hirano retains a number of interesting sites with buildings still extant from the Muromachi period (1336–1568) and thereafter.

Map 5 shows a walking course which begins at Hirano Station, two stops from Tennō-ji on the JR Yamatoji Line. For the most part, the course follows one of Osaka's designated historical walks, identified by brick paving set into the street. The full course, from Tennō-ji station and back, takes about 3 hours.

The presence of many ancient and magnificent broadleaf evergreen and deciduous trees along the route makes late spring ideal for visiting Hirano. The trees will be fully leafed but still fresh, in that vibrant condition the Japanese have given a special name, *wakaba* (literally, "young leaves").

Going south from Hirano Station, the first stop on the walk is Dainembutsu-ji. This temple was founded in 1127 as the headquarters of the Yūzū-nembutsu sect of Buddhism. The massive main image hall, roofed in copper-clad ceramic tiles, is a modern reconstruction, while other buildings date from the Tokugawa period. The grounds also contain several old camphor and gingko trees.

Even more venerable and beautiful are the trees at Kumata Jinja, the next stop on the tour. At the entrance to the shrine compound is a camphor tree more than one thousand years old, and several other impressive specimens of camphor and gingko can be found throughout the site.

The principal buildings have also survived. The inner shrine consists of three thatched structures partly concealed within a walled courtyard at the north end of the shrine compound. The trio of dark, weathered buildings is set in the deep shade of the old trees—especially beautiful on a hot, sunny day. Two of the buildings date from the Muromachi period, and the third is from the Genroku era (1688–1704) of the Tokugawa period. All three are designated Important Cultural Properties.

The shrine also features a wonderful collection of the "lion-dogs" which guard the entrances to many Shinto buildings. These creatures are known in Japanese by various names—*karashishi* ("Chinese lions"), *karainu* ("Chinese dogs"), *komainu* ("Korean dogs")—which indicate confusion about both their species and place of origin. In China and Korea, these sculpted animals are referred to unambiguously as lions, since dogs are considered lowly creatures. In Chinese, the word for dog is used in numerous expressions of contempt (such as the now passé "capitalist running dog").

Linguistic vagaries aside, all the buildings at Kumata Jinja, except one small Inari (the fox god) shrine, have their karashishi. The statues range in age from medieval to modern, in materials from stone to wood to bronze, and in character from dignified to energetic to comical. Their forms and demeanor are variously canine and leonine, reflecting each sculptor's artistic vocabulary, training, or temperament.

A few blocks south of the Kumata Shrine is Senkō-ji, one of the hundreds of Buddhist temples thought to have been founded by Prince Shōtoku. The temple has the further distinction of having been burned in 1576, during the war between Oda Nobunaga and the militant monks of Ishiyama Hongan-ji. Its history is thus peripherally interwoven with two of the main periods in the development of Osaka.

The current Senkō-ji is a small temple whose building dates to the early eighteenth century. One corner of the compound is taken up by a small garden and an unusual grotto-like sculpture court composed of a series of alternating, small-scale images of Jizō under a low roof. Jizō is the patron saint of spirits of the dead, especially of dead children, and his statues are frequently dressed in handmade red aprons and presented with offerings of food and incense. At the feet of many of the Jizō images are brass bells rung to call the deity's attention. The grotto is clearly frequented by many parents and relatives in memory of their lost children, and the atmosphere of quiet pathos is tangible.

The walking route continues east from Senkō-ji rather uneventfully. Several blocks to the east is Hirano Kōen, a park which can kindly be described as nondescript. The park contains a small shrine, the Sanjūbu Jinja, which is an attractive if modest little structure painted an unusually deep crimson. The two historic monuments in the park are the ninth-century burial mound, which looks rather like a pile of discarded stones at the edge of a construction site, and the bamboo-lidded mouth of the well that was the town's original water source, now screened behind a chain-link fence. But don't lose heart now; turning north after crossing the Hirano River and Highway 25, you will soon reach the final, and most impressive, stop on the tour.

Okuda House was home to a family of wealthy farmers who filled the hereditary post of village headman. The main house dates from the early seventeenth century, and has been beautifully preserved. The long, low structure contains some nineteen rooms. The size of the house reflects both the owners' status and the multi-generational nature of family life in premodern Japan. As home of the village headman, Okuda House would have been visited by officials of the local daimyo. As a result, the house contains several rooms which are considerably more elegant than those found in a typical farmhouse. The family's wealth is also evident in the secondary structures within the compound, which include a *kura* (storehouse) for valuables, two granaries, a drying warehouse, and a cotton warehouse. From Okuda House, the tour is completed by the 3-minute walk to the JR Kami Station.

OKUDA HOUSE   (tel. 06-792-2695) 10 A.M. to 4 P.M. the first and third Sunday of every month. Reservations required. Admission: ¥300.

SAKAI AND VICINITY

Sakai is currently Osaka Prefecture's second largest city, and one which rivals the city of Osaka in historical importance. In fact, until the ascension to power of Hideyoshi in 1579, Sakai was the principal city in what is now Osaka Prefecture. It is the location of numerous fifth-century burial mounds, including the grandest of all those built in Japan. During the medieval period, Sakai was Japan's main port of entry for foreign goods and ideas. Emissaries from the Chinese empire, Portugese missionaries, and Dutch traders all passed through the city. It became an autonomous city of merchants, traders, and intellectuals, a center of late-Muromachi-period culture. The decline of Sakai's status and wealth coincided with Osaka's elevation to the status of Japan's economic capital under Hideyoshi's direction.

Sakai is a city highly conscious of and eager to promote its past glories. The municipal government has developed a 7-kilometer walking tour of the historic district called the Teku Teku Road (*tekuteku* is a colloquialism for walking, presumably derived from the sound of footsteps). The route includes the site of tea master Sen no Rikyū's house; a park devoted to Saint Francis Xavier, whose missionary work was based in Sakai; the poet Yosano Akiko's birthplace; and numerous (sixty-seven in all) other historical sites. Unfortunately, these sites are nearly all represented only by stone markers or postwar concrete temple buildings of little visual interest. A few temple gardens and structures of less than outstanding beauty and a merchant house viewable only from the street are meager rewards for 4 hours of tekuteku. As a result, my suggestions for visiting Sakai bypass the former area of the medieval town altogether in favor of more scattered but satisfying sites beyond its edges.

Begin with the oldest and most spectacular of Sakai's monuments, the burial mound of Emperor Nintoku. Take the JR Hanwa Line from Tennō-ji, or the Nankai Line from Namba, to Mikunigaoka Station (you may want to start on an express train and transfer at either the Sakai or Sakai-Higashi Station). The tumulus is unmistakable as a large, tree-covered hill south of the station. As you walk south, along either its west or east side, the vastness of the enterprise required in constructing the tomb becomes increasingly clear, inviting comparisons with the pyramids of Egypt or Central America. The strength of the aspirations, skills, and political organization of preliterate human societies is eloquently expressed in this monumental structure, nearly 500 meters in length.

The traditional identification of this mausoleum, the largest in Japan, as Emperor Nintoku's resting place has largely been accepted by modern scholars. Nintoku's biography, however, was greatly embellished by its chroniclers. According to the earliest written records, the *Nihonshoki* and the *Kojiki*, which were compiled early in the eighth century, Nintoku lived well over a century (either 110 or 143 years, depending on the source), having been conceived when his father was ninety years old. His reign encompassed nearly all the fourth century (313–399). The superhuman scale of Nintoku's achievements is typical of Japan's early histories, and was in part propaganda. Time frames were extended in order to establish the country as an ancient civilization, comparable to China in its past glories.

Nintoku's birth was an inauspicious one. An owl, a bird of ill omen, flew into the room in which he was born. On the same day a wren, considered a lucky bird, flew into the house of the emperor's first minister, to whom a son was also being born. To forestall possible calamity, Emperor Ōjin named his son Osasagi (wren), and gave his minister's son the name Tsuku (owl). The minister presumably accepted this ploy loyally, though the fate of his son is not recorded. Nintoku went on to a brilliant career as sovereign, one of the most popular emperors of ancient Japan. He is credited with having shown great concern for the welfare of his people, promoting agriculture, exempting farmers from taxes for several years, directing the digging of canals and the erection of dikes, and so on. That Nintoku's reign is memorialized in Japan's greatest tumulus is a fitting tribute.

All the remaining Japanese tumuli are now covered in dense vegetation. Most probably, this "natural" condition is contrary to the intention of the builders. Some of the mounds were originally covered by slabs of stone. Haniwa, clay cylinders that were sometimes elaborated and given the form of soldiers, horses, or other figures, were placed in concentric rings around the mounds, probably as guardians. The mausoleum of Nintoku in its current state may appear more beautiful to our eyes, but in its naked form would have been much more clearly a monumental and awe-inspiring human construction.

Because Japan's imperial tradition continues, the mound itself is a consecrated Shinto area, has never been excavated, and is off limits to the public. The chain-link fence surrounding it is an obtrusive element; it is unfortunate also that visitors cannot at least cross the first two moats surrounding it and view the large inner moat and the bulk of the mound itself beyond. A viewing platform has been constructed at the south end, providing the clearest single view of the structure. In addition to Nintoku's tomb, hundreds of other burial mounds dot the landscape around Sakai, some approaching the size of Nintoku's, others smaller than a Japanese mini-car.

Immediately south of Nintoku's tumulus is the main entrance to Daisen Kōen, a large park opened in 1980, and clearly designed as a showpiece for the city. Within the park the Sakai City Museum exhibits artifacts from throughout the city's history. Particularly fine are the exhibits relating to the Tumulus period and earlier prehistoric times, including excavated objects and superb scale models and maps. One model of Nintoku's tomb is particularly useful, as it conveys at least a hint of the mound's original form and power. Some English-language labels are present, though the information contained is skeletal at best. The museum building and its displays are attractive throughout.

The other major feature of Daisen Kōen is its Japanese garden. Like many contemporary gardens in traditional style, it may be guilty of trying too hard—combining too many different elements into one landscape. Nevertheless, many of the elements are unusual and quite beautifully realized, rarely crossing over into the stale stereotyping of many contemporary gardens. The large resthouse near the garden entrance is a fine modern interpretation of classic wooden construction, and makes an excellent shelter for a short rest or a picnic lunch. Chinese-style pavilions in the garden are symbolic of Sakai's long history of cultural and mercantile ties to that country. The Chinese elements are unfortunate intrusions into the garden. Their

SAKAI AND VICINITY

design shows considerably less confidence and imagination than the Japanese motifs.

Across the highway south of Daisen Kōen is a city-owned center of a type often translated as a "greening center." Its purpose is to encourage citizens to plant more trees and shrubs as a means of improving the quality of the local environment. Whether such centers have the desired effect or not, they certainly provide an island of flourishing plant life. Sakai's greening center, designed by the renowned architectural firm Sakakura Associates, consists of an interesting if somewhat chaotic sequence of buildings and spaces, all filled with a profusion of green and flowering plants.

My suggested explorations of Sakai City have so far skirted both the downtown with its historical fragments and the heavily industrial districts which fuel its modern economy. This apparent anti-urban tendency continues with two other sites located a few kilometers from Sakai proper.

Mozu Station on the JR Hanwa Line is about 200 meters east of Daisen Kōen. Three stops further south on this line is Ōtori Station, and from the station a 400-meter walk north will bring you to Ōtori Taisha. This shrine is considered a milestone in the evolution of Shinto architecture, more sophisticated than the earliest known forms, represented by Ise and Izumo, and predating the next major development represented by Osaka's Sumiyoshi Taisha.

The origins of all these early shrines are obscure. In the cases of Ise, Izumo, and Sumiyoshi there are at least myths regarding their beginnings and traditional (though apocryphal) dates assigned to the events. Concerning Ōtori Taisha, however, not even a legend remains. In ninth-century documents it is recorded as one of the Grand Shrines, but its status as one of Japan's oldest is based solely on the style of the buildings themselves. The Ōtori style differs from that of the earlier shrines in that the main sanctuary's width has been increased from two to three bays, eliminating the pillar in the middle of the facade and permitting a central entrance porch. This pattern would be followed in later developments, including the Sumiyoshi style.

Such scholarly niceties aside, Ōtori Taisha's principal sanctuary is a beautiful structure set amidst a cluster of ancient and moss-covered trees. Although the wooden fence around the building prevents close study of the architectural details, the building's impressive scale and dignified character make it well worth visiting. The fact that the shrine is little known outside the ranks of architectural historians, and therefore unlikely to be included on many package tours, makes the trek all the more special.

Elsewhere on the grounds of the Ōtori Taisha are two Japanese gardens, both enjoyable but both in need of maintenance. The shrine's fortunes seem to be on the upswing, perhaps due to the development and promotion of its facilities for wedding ceremonies, an enterprise that many hotels and other private companies have certainly found lucrative. In any case, a considerable amount of renovation work is in progress at the shrine; the iris garden, the more interesting of the two landscaped spaces, appears to be the focus of some needed attention.

If you are seeking dramatic floral displays, it might be better to wait until mid- to late June to visit Sakai. The irises will be past their peak, but the rose gardens at Hamadera Kōen will be in full bloom. Hamadera Kōen is 2 kilometers or so west of Ōtori Taisha's west entrance. A visit to the taxi stand at the shrine entrance will save you a 20-minute walk of no sightseeing value whatsoever, and by this time you will welcome any opportunity to get off your feet.

Hamadera Kōen has the distinction of being Japan's oldest public park, established in 1873. Much of the park's layout has been changed dramatically over the years, but a formal promenade leading west from the main entrance has a distinctly Victorian-era feeling about it, especially when you reach the fountains and geometrically arranged rose garden. Considerably more lush and extensive than Osaka's famed Nakanoshima rose garden, this European-style display is just a prelude to a truly surprising garden within its own fenced compound just south of the promenade.

Bara Teien (literally "rose garden") is a Japanese-style stroll garden which uses the rose, a distinctly alien flower, as its primary motif. Ponds, streams, gravel beds, and other features are presented in a fairly traditional manner, but the center of the space is dominated by lavish beds of roses in all sizes and colors. The roses are organized into an abstracted version of a terraced mountainside, the rich green expected in such a landscape replaced by intense layers of contrasting colors. The recently completed garden is, to my knowledge, the only one of its type in the world, and its beauty both reinforced my appreciation for the continuing development of the Japanese landscaping tradition and caused me to reconsider a Western flower whose attraction had previously escaped me.

Roses and promenade aside, Hamadera Kōen is more a park for family recreation than a tourist attraction. It contains a large ameboid swimming complex and an amusement park similar to those found on department store rooftops in Japanese cities. The best course of action is to retrace your steps from Bara Teien to the main entrance and continue a few short blocks east to the Nankai Hamadera Station. The station itself is another pleasant surprise—a Western-style wood-framed structure dating to 1907, and kept in excellent condition. From here, a local train will take you to Sakai Station for transfer to an express ride of 10 minutes back to Namba.

The full course described above is a busy day's touring, and if undertaken on a muggy summer day may leave you more than a little tired. If your main interest is in greenery and an escape from the city, you may want to start the tour in reverse, leaving open the option of dropping out before the museum and Nintoku's burial mound. The true history buff may choose to follow the city's designated walking course (maps are available at City Hall, just south of the Sakai-Higashi Station on the Nankai Kōya Line). Please don't try to do both their course and mine in one day; that's too much tekuteku for anyone.

DAISEN KŌEN Always open.

SAKAI CITY MUSEUM 9:30 A.M. to 5 P.M. Closed Mondays, national holidays, and December 28 to January 4. Admission: ¥200.

JAPANESE GARDEN 9:30 A.M. to 5 P.M. Closed Mondays, national holidays, and December 28 to January 4. Admission: ¥200.

SAKAI CITY GREENING CENTER 9:30 A.M. to 5 P.M. Closed Mondays, national holidays, and December 28 to January 4. Admission: free.

HAMADERA KŌEN Always open.

BARA TEIEN 10 A.M. to 5 P.M. from March 1 to November 30. Closed Wednesdays and national holidays. Admission: free.

TONDABAYASHI CITY

Tondabayashi City is located south of Osaka on the Kintetsu Nagano Line. From the Kintetsu Abenobashi Station, it is a 35-minute ride by local express train (*junkyū*).

Tondabayashi's history is closely tied to the origins of the modern city of Osaka. The priests of Hongan-ji, having established their headquarters in Osaka, set out in the mid-sixteenth century to extend their political and religious influence into the countryside. In the process, they established several new towns, of which Tondabayashi's Jinai-machi (literally, "town within the temple") is one. During a time of little central governmental control, these towns became semi-autonomous mini-states allied to the main temple of Hongan-ji.

Jinai-machi was surrounded by a modest fortification of mounded earth, a partial moat, and densely planted hedges. Within its confines, a community of artisans and merchants developed and thrived. Although no sixteenth-century buildings survive, Jinai-machi contains many eighteenth- and nineteenth-century houses and two premodern temples. The original street layout has been preserved, and new buildings in the district maintain the scale, if not the architectural style, of the old city.

Jinai-machi begins about 200 meters south of Tondabayashi Station. A stroll of 1 or 2 hours through its streets will take you past many fine old *machiya* (townhouses), and give a good sense of the scale of a Tokugawa-period town. The older houses and temples are identified and a walking course is suggested on a Japanese-language map available at the visitor center attached to the train station. Most of the old machiya in Jinai-machi are still occupied, in some cases by descendants of the original owners, and are not open to the public. The modern residents' requirements for electricity, sanitary plumbing, and other amenities have resulted in alterations to both the individual dwellings and the streetscape in general. Sometimes annoying, these modern intrusions nonetheless make clear that Jinai-machi is a living town rather than a museum diorama.

Near the southwest edge of the area is the Sugiyama Residence, one of the oldest and grandest of Jinai-machi's machiya. It was built over several generations, with the oldest remaining section, the earth-floored entrance and workroom called the *doma,* dating from the mid-seventeenth century. The remainder of the house, including living quarters and garden, was built in the early eighteenth century. The Sugiyama Residence has been restored to its original condition and opened to visitors. It is a beautiful example of a Tokugawa-period merchant house, complete with walls and fusuma (sliding doors) painted by Kano school artists, elegant carpentry details, and a pleasant landscape garden. The house is designated as an Important Cultural Property.

Directly across the street from the Sugiyama Residence is the recently opened Jinai-machi Museum. It features displays and artifacts related to the town's history.

Also within Tondabayashi City is the Nishikiori Jinja, which contains another building designated as an Important Cultural Property. This shrine building was constructed in 1363, and the style of its roof construction is said to be unique. In any case, the shrine is a lovely old structure which exhibits the fine patina of age. Its wooden beams, rafters, and brackets carry faded traces of a once-elaborate paint scheme, perhaps garish when fresh but now pleasantly muted. Nishikiori Jinja is most easily reached from Kawanishi Station, from which it is a 5-minute walk.

Another historical monument in the Tondabayashi area is Ryūsen-ji, reached by bus or taxi from Tondabayashi Station. This temple features a famous but ill-maintained landscape garden. The garden was designed to represent the Buddhist paradise, but while its basic form remains, the current appearance of the garden is far from heavenly. The temple also contains a Niō-mon (Deva gate), built in 1275, which is an Important Cultural Property. The gate is unusual in style, preserving elements of Nara-period (645–794) construction, though built much later. Ryūsen-ji is certainly worth a visit if you're interested in Buddhist architecture, and its mountain-side location is picturesque.

In Tondabayashi City you can't help but notice an impressive but bizarre tower on the edge of the city. The Peace Tower dominates views of the area. It was built by the Church of Perfect Liberty as a monument to world peace in 1970, and has been recently renovated.

SUGIYAMA RESIDENCE   10 A.M. to 5 P.M. Closed Mondays.

JINAI-MACHI MUSEUM   10 A.M. to 5 P.M. Closed Mondays.

PEACE TOWER   9 A.M. to 4 P.M. Closed Wednesdays. Admission: ¥200.

KAWACHI NAGANO

The hidden treasure of Osaka Prefecture lies in the foothills of the Kongō mountain range, near the Wakayama Prefecture border. The hills around the city contain numerous sites, natural and historical, which equal in beauty and significance many of the better-known attractions elsewhere in the Kansai district. It is a bit off the beaten path, and its attractions are not concentrated in a way that makes for convenience in touring, but the rewards will more than justify your efforts. I have given directions based on using public transportation, as I have throughout the book, but this is one area where renting a cab or a car for the day may be worth considering.

Even if you drive, start at the Kawachi Nagano Station to get oriented and pick up the map/brochure (in English and Japanese) at the tourist information booth. The station is on the Nankai Kōya Line, originating at Namba, a 30-minute ride by express train. From the station, all the places mentioned below may be reached by bus or by local train, and visiting them all may require several returns to the station to make the necessary changes of buses and train routes. It will also require several days if you wish to take in both the scenic and historic sites. A final note about public transportation in the Kawachi Nagano region: buses on several of the routes are infrequent, so check the posted return schedules whenever you get off a bus if you intend to continue or return on the same route.

The history of the Kawachi Nagano area is a rich one, tied to some of Japan's most famous events and leaders. It is most fully embodied at Amanosan Kongō-ji, a temple nestled in a beautiful valley southwest of the city (a 20-minute bus ride from Kawachi Nagano Station). Its origins are in the Nara period, but Kongō-ji became a major religious center in the Heian period, when it adopted the creed of Shingon Buddhism introduced to Japan by the priest Kūkai, also known as Kōbō (Saint) Daishi.

Kūkai's renown as a leader in the development of Japanese Buddhism is second only to that of Prince Shōtoku (see chapter on Shitennō-ji, page 45). Like the prince, Kūkai's influence extended into the secular realm as well. Kūkai was the inventor of hiragana, the first Japanese syllabary, which was a breakthrough that led to incalculable changes in literature and literacy during the Heian period and thereafter. But Kūkai's main mission was the establishment of a new sect of Buddhism, called Shingon, meaning "true word," which Kūkai had studied in China between 804 and 806.

He began preaching his faith in Kyoto, but soon found the political intrigues of the imperial court distracting and potentially dangerous. The Shingon sect became involved in a sort of power struggle for imperial approval with the Tendai sect, established in Japan just two years prior to Kūkai's return from China. Tendai had established a headquarters on Mt. Hiei, north of the capital, and Kūkai sought a similar mountain retreat on which to build a center for Shingon meditation. In 816 he chose Mt. Kōya (Kōya-san), in modern Wakayama Prefecture, not far south of Osaka. Kōya-san gradually developed into the largest and most beautiful of Japan's mountain temples, the destination of many pilgrimages up to the present day. At its height, there were some one thousand temple buildings on the mountain.

Along the pilgrimage route to Kōya-san many temples grew to serve the needs of the travelers, and Kongō-ji became one of the most important of these. For doctrinal reasons, women were not permitted on Mt. Kōya itself, and Kongō-ji became the final destination for most female pilgrims of the Shingon faith, perhaps because of its proximity to the holy mountain. As Shingon's center for the religious instruction of women, Kongō-ji earned the nickname "the women's Kōya-san."

Kongō-ji's place in the religious history of Japan is balanced by its role in the political events of the Nambokuchō period (1336–1392), when the imperial court was divided into competing southern and northern factions. This period of civil warfare occupied most of the fourteenth century, and the shifts of power and loyalties, the exiles and restorations of its principal players, are exceedingly complex. The core of the struggle was an attempt to return actual governmental power to the emperor, who had long since become a mere puppet of the Kamakura shogunate. The period has become deeply ingrained in the Japanese consciousness, drenched in the romantic fatalism that accrues to noble but hopeless causes. Legend has it that one of the principals, Kusunoki Masashige, heading into certain death in battle, urged his ten-year-old son to remember the cause and remain loyal to it. During the later stages of the Second World War, a song based on this incident became popular with Japanese troops; it was banned during the Allied occupation. In a more contemporary vein, the period was the subject of an enormously popular mini-series on NHK in 1991.

Kawachi Nagano's connection to the events of the Nambokuchō period are the result of the clan which controlled the region at the time, the Kusunoki. Kusunoki Masashige, the early fourteenth-century subject of the song alluded to above, became Emperor Go-Daigo's main military supporter during the latter's attempt to restore imperial power. From shortly after his ascension in 1331, Go-Daigo was in exile for two years at the command of the shogunate. Masashige and his allies, who had declared loyalty to the emperor, fought the Kamakura armies and built two castles, Akasaka and Chikaya, on the flanks of Mt. Kongō above Kawachi Nagano. (The sites of the castles are marked by memorial stones, but the scant remains make the rather arduous trek to visit them a disappointment.)

From 1333 to 1335, Go-Daigo's forces held the throne, only to be ousted and sent into exile again by the treachery of the warlord Ashikaga Takauji. Masashige's troops continued to resist until a decisive battle in the modern Kobe area. Masashige knew his forces would lose, but loyally followed Go-Daigo's orders not to withdraw. After a desperate battle in which he was wounded eleven times, Masashige was forced to commit suicide.

Go-Daigo escaped once more from captivity and fled to Yoshino, in the mountains of Nara Prefecture southeast of Kawachi Nagano, where he established his southern court as a rival to Kyoto. The divided court continued for fifty years after Go-Daigo's death, with his descendants occupying the southern throne and Masashige's descendants filling the role of military supporters.

And now at last we can return to Kongō-ji, for this temple became a secondary palace for the emperors of the southern court. Located in the heart of the Kusunoki clan's territory, the temple was relatively secure; since it was in the foothills, at a considerably lower elevation than Yoshino, its climate was much more benign, especially in winter. Much of the architecture which remains at Kongō-ji today was built during the Nambokuchō period, no doubt to provide the emperor with a suitably regal setting. Two of the buildings were constructed expressly as imperial residences, and it is with those buildings that this tour will begin.

The larger of the two residences is the Okuden. Although it has the features of a detached palace, it actually functioned more as a prison. In 1351, Go-Murakami, son and successor to Go-Daigo as leader of the southern court, launched an attack on Kyoto and captured the current northern emperor and two of his retired predecessors. In 1354 they came to reside at Kongō-ji's Okuden. Both the name Okuden, meaning "hidden palace," and its standard description as the "northern court's temporary headquarters" are thus euphemistic.

The Okuden's design contains no hint of a prison. It is a small, simple structure, but all the more compelling for its modest scale, and exudes the dignity which must have been afforded Go-Murakami's imperial rivals. The building is entered from a modern covered passageway which affords views of a marvelous landscape garden, rebuilt in the fifteenth century. Through the garden you will glimpse the Okuden, a thatch-roofed structure, nearly square in plan.

The main room within is an audience hall, which had its origins in the aristocratic residences of the Heian period, called *shinden*. Although this room is now floored completely in tatami, this was in fact a later alteration. Originally, the floors were exposed wood, with mats placed only where the captive emperor and his visitors were seated. The highest mat was reserved for the emperor, whose portion of the room was separated from the rest by a wooden transom and bamboo curtains. This room-within-a-room is called a *jōdan-no-ma*, and is a distinguishing characteristic of the style of aristocratic residence which would develop throughout the next three centuries, the *shoin* style. The Okuden contains other progressive elements as well. The use of flat ceilings is unlike older shinden-style residences, where the rooms were generally open to the rafters and roof structures above. Even more striking is the use of shoji on the exterior of the building, replacing the hinged wooden shutters used in the earlier style.

The Mani-in, also known as "the southern court's temporary headquarters," was built for the use of Go-Murakami, who resided there from 1354 to 1360, and whose successors also made use of the residence over the next three decades. In it, additional features of the shoin style are present. The term "shoin" originally referred to a room used as a study in a Buddhist priest's residence, but came to describe a style of residential architecture in which shoin-type spaces were included. Principal features of the room included a window located in one corner and a low wooden sill which served as a desk. The Mani-in's shoin window is an early and quite beautiful example. Later versions of the shoin window were strictly decorative, and were combined with the tokonoma alcove and other elements into a standardized composition. But here the shoin is a true writing alcove, complete with knee space underneath. Also interesting is the use of fusuma sliding panels as room dividers. Heian palaces used some sliding door panels, but most room dividers were either movable screens or roll-down bamboo curtains like those seen in the Okuden. At Mani-in the system of floor tracks and overhead guides used in moving the fusuma is unusually complicated, an experimental version that would be superceded as the style evolved.

The Mani-in also features a small but lovely garden, whose main plant is the bush clover, or *hagi*. The story told of this plant's unusual predominance in the garden is that it was a favorite food of horses, and Emperor Go-Murakami was particularly fond of horses. Thus the garden was planted in hagi to ensure that the emperor's mounts did not stray too far from the palace.

Both imperial residences at Kongō-ji are superb architectural monuments, beautiful in their own right, important as milestones in the development of Japanese architecture, and eloquent as expressions of the time and circumstances of their construction. Their remote, rural setting and humble scale convey the sense of a retreat much more convincingly than does the opulent, self-conciously rustic style of their more famous descendants at

Katsura and Shūgaku-in in Kyoto. The buildings' modesty also expresses the real poverty, in relative terms of course, of the southern court. A visit to Kongō-ji's detached palaces may make the romanticism of the Nambokuchō period more tangible if you are not already steeped in its history.

The residences are located just north of the walled compound of the temple proper. This compound includes several buildings from the fourteenth century, some of which were extensively repaired in the seventeenth century. Together, the assemblage is the best medieval temple compound remaining in Osaka Prefecture. One structure is even earlier in date; the Kondō, or Golden Hall, was likely built in the late twelfth century. Like the imperial residences, the Kondō is a rare example of a transitional architectural style. Generally based on older Chinese forms, it features a sweeping, curved roof projection which acts as a porch. This porch was clearly an amenity for the pilgrims who came to worship here, but its origins are less apparent. Probably the form originated in Japanese palatial architecture somewhat earlier, but its appearance at Kongō-ji is the earliest to have been preserved in a temple setting. The porch gives the building a magnanimous, welcoming quality and makes it the focus of the compound.

The Shōmon, or main gate, is an impressive and well-preserved entrance to the compound. To the left of the gate is a pond and three small Shinto shrines, indicative of both the syncretism of Kūkai's religious doctrine and the imperial patronage enjoyed by the temple. Opposite the shrines is the Ama-no-den, a rather delicate-looking structure in which Go-Murakami conducted affairs of state while in residence at Kongō-ji.

Opposite the Kondō is the Tahōtō, a pagoda which is associated in style with Shingon Buddhism. A set of stairs behind the Tahōtō leads to another group of buildings, later in date and lesser in beauty.

Still further, the steps lead up the mountainside, becoming a trail dotted with small statues of the Bodhisattva Kannon (Avalokitesvara), each under its own roofed shelter. This trail is a version in miniature of one of Japan's most famous pilgrimage routes—to the thirty-three Kannon temples. The full version of the pilgrimage involves traveling all over the Kansai district, from Hikone in the north to Himeji in the west to Kōya-san in the south.

(Modern pilgrims can do the circuit in a sixteen-day bus tour, probably as taxing in its own way as the old-fashioned hiking method.) The scaled-down route at Kongō-ji was thought to convey the same spiritual merit as the original course at a discount in time and effort. The mini-pilgrimage at Kongō-ji seems to smack of paternalism, given the temple's place as "the women's Kōya-san"; the ladies, it would seem, couldn't be expected to exert themselves as vigorously as males in their spiritual quests. But in fairness I should note that similar trails exist at other temples which were not especially associated with women.

Before leaving Kongō-ji, visit the Hōmotsukan (Treasure Hall), a modern building which displays Kongō-ji's small but fine collection of sculpture and paintings, as well as numerous historic artifacts of the Nambokuchō period. A pair of screen paintings from the Muromachi period is a designated National Treasure. These screens depict landscapes, one featuring the sun, the other the moon.

The style of the paintings ties nicely into the temple's history. Yamato-e is the native Japanese style in the arts that first flourished in the later Heian period, and is often thought of as the feminine side of Japanese culture. In literature, Yamato-e is represented by Lady Murasaki's *Tale of Genji,* the famous novel which was written in the Japanese vernacular (a style made possible by Kōbō Daishi's invention of the hiragana syllabary). In painting, the style is highly decorative, brilliantly colored, and evocative rather than realistic. During the Kamakura period the Yamato-e style fell from favor, and its revival at various times in Japan's later history, as in the *Sun and Moon Landscapes,* was usually indicative of a nostalgia for the days of direct imperial rule, a sentiment tragically embodied in the history of Go-Daigo and Kusunoki Masashige.

Closely related to Kongō-ji is another spectacular temple, Kanshin-ji. It may also be reached by bus from Kawachi Nagano Station, a 10-minute ride. The Kanshin-ji bus stops are not immediately adjacent to the temple. If the bus turns a corner just before stopping, return to the road you were on before the turn and continue uphill about 200 meters; if the bus doesn't turn, the stop will still be about 100 meters short of the temple entrance.

Kanshin-ji is a smaller complex than Kongō-ji, but its mountainside site is even more beautiful. The centerpiece of Kanshin-ji is its Kondō, a National Treasure dating from the fourteenth century. It is similar to Kongō-ji's Kondō in that it features a porch-like extension of its tiled roof, but the porch here is larger and more elaborate. Its scale is magnified by the nature of the approach to the Kondō: you climb a long flight of steps directly in front of the building, thus first viewing the sweeping porch roof from below. Kanshin-ji's Kondō is painted in the Chinese style, which further increases its grandeur.

Inside the Kondō is a layout peculiar to temples of the Shingon sect. A brief detour into the nature of Shingon practices will help illuminate this dark and rather mysterious sanctuary.

Shingon is one of the esoteric sects of Buddhism. Its rites and teachings were only gradually revealed to its adherents through long years of instruction and meditation. The most sacred and secret of the doctrines were not entrusted to written form, but passed down orally from the masters only to their most accomplished disciples. The uninitiated faithful were invited to worship, but were denied access to these secret truths.

The Shingon cosmos was populated by an array of Buddhas, each representing a different aspect of the perfect whole, and all of them subservient to the ultimate Buddha-nature represented by the Buddha Dainichi (Vairocana). The universe could also be seen as a duality of essence, or spirit, and phenomena, or material. The cosmic order was expressed visually in the mandala form, either two- or three-dimensional representations of the order of the universe. The full understanding of the mandala was again reserved for initiates, but the images were a prominent feature of sanctuaries like that at Kanshin-ji.

Peering into the sanctuary inside the Kondō from behind a latticed wall, one first sees a group of tables containing offerings to the deities, and benches at which the priests conduct their rituals. Flanking this group are two large wall panels on which are painted representations of the most common Shingon mandalas. The Diamond World is the world of essence, the Womb World opposite it is the world of phenomena. These intricate and sublime paintings are darkened with centuries of incense smoke, and are barely visible from the vantage point permitted to most visitors. Behind the altar are the hall's most sacred and famous images, but these are completely hidden, locked behind black lacquered doors except for two days a year, April 17 and 18, when the doors are opened for about forty minutes or so to air the chamber. For these brief periods, visitors flock to the temple in droves to catch a glimpse of the statues.

The mandalas were presumably painted at the time of the construction of the Kondō, but the central sculptured image is of much earlier date. The Nyoirin Kannon is a product of the Heian period, dated 836. It is a truly strange and unique work of art. The six-armed figure sits in a pose which is simultaneously relaxed and carefully controlled. Its face is similarly ambiguous, appearing soft and lackadaisical one moment, intensely taut and focused the next.

All these images can best be seen in photographs (available for viewing and purchase at the temple), but the atmosphere of the sanctuary as a whole can only be appreciated in person. When we visited Kanshin-ji, the office was presided over by an ancient but very lively priest. Our Japanese was slightly better than his English, and after a brief discussion revealed our familiarity with the temple and its treasures, the priest led us through a side door into the sanctuary itself (rather to the shock of the Japanese visitors outside as well as to ourselves). We were able to see the altar and the mandala paintings at close range, but the doors to the Nyoirin Kannon's sanctum remained closed.

Our discussions with the priest yielded some valuable information as well. He pointed out that the larger and more famous religious complexes on Mt. Kōya and at Yoshino, as well as urban temples like Shitennō-ji, had suffered much more destruction due to fire than had Kanshin-ji and Kongō-ji. Indeed, Kōya-san has only one building predating the oldest of Kongō-ji's structures, in spite of its much grander history. The reason the priest gave for this is that the location of Kawachi Nagano is virtually ideal: it is too far from the major cities to have suffered from warfare and frequent fires, but sufficiently low in elevation, in the foothills rather than the mountain peaks, to have been spared the lightning-induced fires which repeatedly devastated other mountain temples.

It is fortunate that the warfare of the Nambokuchō period never reached the area. In fact, Kanshin-ji had the strongest of ties to Kusunoki Masashige, and is his burial place. To one side of the Kondō is a small, thatch-roofed building, the Tatekake-no-tō, which was built as a monument to Masashige's troops who died in battle in the attempt to restore Emperor Go-Daigo to power. The word "tō" in the structure's name means "pagoda," though this building is unlike any other pagoda of which I am aware, consisting of a single story rather than the usual three or five. It is a satisfying little structure, delicate and monumental at once, its elaborate bracketing contrasting nicely with the simple hipped roof above.

After Kongō-ji and Kanshin-ji, the remaining historic sites around Kawachi Nagano may seem anticlimactic, but still they are worth pursuing. Continuing into the hills on the same route which brought you to Kanshin-ji for an additional 10-minute bus ride will bring you to the Kami-kobuka bus stop and the Yamamoto family farmhouse. This seventeenth-century *minka* has been beautifully restored and maintained. While open-air museums, such as the one at Hattori Ryokuchi Kōen (page 107), offer the chance to see a variety of old farmhouses in one place, it is rare to find a minka preserved and open to the public on its original site.

Another possible destination from Kanshin-ji is Enmei-ji, a temple famed for its autumn foliage. One gnarled and moss-covered maple tree here is said to be one thousand years old. A trail from the main temple compound leads to a grove of maples surrounding a lotus pond. The route from Kanshin-ji to Enmei-ji is a broad hiking trail through hillsides of cedar and bamboo, about a 20-minute walk. From Enmei-ji, a further 40-minute downhill walk will bring you to Mikkaichichō Station on the Nankai Kōya Line.

Two local stops further south on the train line is Amami Station, home to the best-known hot springs in the area, the Amami Onsen. A traditional stop for weary pilgrims on their way to Mt. Kōya, the onsen today has lodgings for seventy guests and is said to be popular among visitors from nearby Osaka.

Visitors interested in scenic rather than historical sites will find that the hills around Kawachi Nagano offer a variety of worthy choices. Hiking trails are to be found in abundance. Trails may be picked up near both the Yamamoto farmhouse and Amami Onsen, but the prime location for embarking on a trek into the woods is in the vicinity of the Takihata Reservoir. Buses run to the reservoir from Kawachi Nagano Station. The stop farthest from the city is called Takihata Dam, but is really at the south end of the lake, opposite the dam. From here, numerous hiking trails branch off. Some take you to several of the "48 Waterfalls" in the area. Another is the Diamond Trail, developed by the prefectural government and roughly following the ridge line of the Kongō mountain range. Following this trail east for several kilometers, you will reach Mt. Iwawaki, one of the tallest peaks in the area. The summit is covered in miscanthus grass (*kaya*), the material used in thatched roofs. The waving field of grass is beautiful, an unusual sight in Japan, and also permits an amazing 360-degree view of the surrounding countryside. All of the hiking trails in the Kawachi Nagano region are shown on the detailed map/brochure in English and Japanese available at the Kawachi Nagano Station's tourist information booth.

With so many features to recommend it, it is a wonder that Kawachi Nagano is not overrun with tourists. That it is not is another reason visiting the area is such a joy.

KONGŌ-JI   9 A.M. to 4:30 P.M. (tel. 0721-52-5832). Admission: ¥300. Mani-in open weekends only.

KANSHIN-JI   9 A.M. to 5 P.M. (tel. 0721-62-2134). Admission: ¥100, additional fee for Kondō.

OSAKA HARBOR

Osaka's port area covers a long stretch of coastline. From Hokkō (north harbor), where the pleasure yachts of the elite are moored, down to the site of the future Kansai International Airport (scheduled to open in 1994), is a straight-line distance of some 40 kilometers. As noted in the history chapter this coastline is entirely artificial, the result of dredging and land reclamation projects that have been proceeding for over a century.

While the coastline modifications have been aimed at trade and industrial expansion, there is also a history of recreational development of the port. Tempōzan, the focus of contemporary tourist developments at the port, is also the historic origin of such developments. The name Tempōzan refers to an artificial mountain (*zan*) created during the Tempō era (1830–1844) of the Tokugawa period. The "mountain" was the result of dredging operations in the adjacent Yodo River shipping channel—then, as now, one of the principal entry points from the harbor. The hill was landscaped, complete with teahouse, lanterns, and bridges, and the populace was invited to come there for enjoyment; it became a prototype public park. Tempōzan's popularity is suggested by its inclusion in nineteenth-century prints of famous Osaka places. Today's Tempōzan Kōen bears little resemblance to the old prints, its mountain shrunken to a small hill, though it is easily identifiable as the only green space in the district. It is a nondescript little park significant only for its history.

Today's recreational attractions, grouped together as Tempōzan Harbor Village, are even easier to locate: take the Chūō subway line to its western terminus, Osaka-kō Station, and follow the crowds.

The centerpiece of the district today is the Kaiyūkan (Osaka Aquarium), also called the Ring of Fire, a huge state-of-the-art facility of the highest caliber. It was designed by Cambridge Seven, the U.S. firm that has designed many aquaria, including Boston's. "Ring of Fire" is a phrase describing the Pacific Rim, an unbroken circle of volcanic and seismic activity, which also contains a number of distinct marine environments that are the theme of the aquarium's displays. This theme is carried out clearly and dramatically in a series of multi-storied tanks connected by a roughly spiral ramp and surrounding the giant central tank. The latter, representing the heart of the Pacific Ocean, is currently the world's largest.

The building is beautifully planned to handle the large crowds anticipated, but long waits were still the norm well over a year after its opening. I spent more time than I cared to standing outside and contemplating the mosaic mural on the building's facade, designed by the principal architect, Alexander Chermakoff. On the whole, the building is architecturally satisfying, its displays spectacular, and its crowd-control system admirable.

After visiting the aquarium, with its pristine seawater imported from far offshore in the Pacific Ocean, a ride on Tempōzan's sightseeing boat will bring you back to the gritty reality of Osaka Harbor. The *Santa Maria* is a "replica" of Columbus's flagship—complete with a steel plate hull, diesel engines, and a pilot house grafted onto the decorative main mast. Of course, Columbus's connection with Osaka is no less tenuous than the boat is authentic; I also doubt that his crew was entertained with cocktails and flamenco dancers below deck.

Anachronistic trappings aside, the *Santa Maria* cruise is real enough, and the harbor is worth a visit. The recent construction along the cruise route includes two impressive bridges: Hokkō Renraku Kyōbashi is a delicate cable suspension bridge, and Minato Ōhashi is a massive red lattice of steel. Shipping facilities include the Tempōzan ferry terminal and the Benten-chō passenger terminal, where ocean liners dock on their visits to Osaka. Industrial trade facilities consist mainly of gleaming new containership docks, with their strangely zoomorphic mobile cranes (at rest, the cranes look like giant mechanical coyotes howling silently). Along with the impressive new facilities are a few remnants of Osaka's older industrial style—dark, grim jumbles of machinery, metal sheds, and piled coal. And throughout the cruise, the polluted waters of the harbor, almost black alongside the boat, reveal the consequences of Osaka's uncontrolled industrial development and the work remaining to be done in transforming the waterfront into a healthy environment.

After the cruise, or while waiting for your departure time after buying

OSAKA HARBOR

tickets, visit the Tempōzan Marketplace. Modeled on American "festival markets" such as Boston's Quincy Market and San Francisco's Ghirardelli Square, it features upscale shops loosely connected by maritime and international themes: African clothing and European teddy bears are among the offerings. There is also a food court which includes the newly emerging Japanese-style fast-food franchises—such as Corocoro, the Rice-Ball Shop—as well as the usual burger, pizza, and ice-cream chains.

Leaving Tempōzan via Osaka-kō Station, a two-stop subway ride brings you to Benten-chō, where the large ocean-going pleasure liners dock. This pier is about 700 meters northwest of the subway station.

Also in Benten-chō is a complex, still under construction in 1993, called Osaka Resort City (ORC—pronounced ōku). Japan's attempts to transform into a leisure-oriented society may be most visible here. One of the completed buildings is known as Paradiso and consists of three floors of entertainment facilities, from a bowling alley on the lowest level to a swimming complex under the translucent fabric of the roof. In between are the Tour of the Universe, a simulated space-travel fantasy (using technology and a copyrighted program developed in Canada), and Fly Away, a cylindrical room with a giant fan at the bottom in which customers in padded suits can experience something resembling a parachutist's free fall. The swimming complex includes water slides, rapids, and a lap pool suspended in midair like a highway overpass. Each of the thrills has a steep ticket price. Paradiso is two blocks north of the subway station, on the west side of the elevated highway.

On the opposite side of the highway is the Benten-chō Station on the JR loop line, and connected to its north end is the Modern Transportation Museum. Modern times seem very old-fashioned after a visit to ORC, but this museum will interest children and railroad buffs with its combination of historical and hands-on displays. English labels are not to be found, but the real fun is in climbing through the old steam engines and watching the model trains go around.

Outside the central harbor area, the yacht club of Hokkō is accessible by city bus #56 from the Nishiku-jō Station on the JR loop line for weekend sailors. Public transportation access to Hokkō may be expected to improve with the eventual completion of Sports Island, which will make Paradiso look primitive. Sports Island will contain a year-round indoor ski slope; baseball, tennis, and other athletic facilities; and, perhaps strangest of all, camping areas . . . with simulated campfires for cooking your meals?

Since we seem to be surrounded by simulated environments, I'll mention the swimming beach at Nankō (southern harbor). Here seawater is filtered and "purified" before being pumped into a pool behind a levee which separates it from the harbor. An imported sand beach, palm trees, and a wave-making machine complete the scene. I have reservations about the water quality at the quasi-beach, but am staggered at the fact that the same levee is used as a fishing park by anglers pulling fish out of the unfiltered, unpurified waters of the harbor opposite the beach. The remainder of Nankō consists mainly of a large housing complex and a commercial district centered on INTEX Osaka, a vast convention center. The Nankō Yachō Kōen (Wild Bird Sanctuary), discussed in a later chapter (page 117), is located in this area.

Finally, I should mention the forthcoming Kansai International Airport, on an artificial island off the coast of southern Osaka Prefecture. Assuming that ground transportation improvements keep pace with airport construction, the new facility should make international access to Osaka much easier. The project has been long-anticipated, and beset by problems ranging from political (pressure to open up construction bids to foreign companies) to technical (the island showed a distressing tendency to sink into the seabed below). Currently scheduled to open in 1994, the terminal, designed by the French architect Renzo Piano, and operating twenty-four hours a day, will be a tangible contribution to Osaka's self-proclaimed internationalism.

OSAKA AQUARIUM ("RING OF FIRE") 1-1-10 Kaiga-dōri, Minato-ku, Osaka (tel. 06-576-5500). 10 A.M. to 8 P.M. Closed every third Wednesday from December through February and on December 31. Admission: ¥1,950.

SANTA MARIA **HARBOR CRUISES** Tempōzan Harbor Village (tel. 06-942-5511). Boat leaves on the hour from 11 A.M. to 5 P.M. (45-minute cruise).

Closed in December and every third Wednesday from January through February. Fare: ¥1,200. Night cruises: April 1 to October 31 at 7 P.M. (2 hours). Night cruise fare: ¥2,500.

PARADISO   Each attraction costs ¥2,000 to ¥3,000.

MODERN TRANSPORTATION MUSEUM   Minato-ku, Osaka (tel. 06-581-5771). 9:30 A.M. to 5 P.M. Closed Mondays. Admission: ¥260.

NATURE

PARKS

Osaka's modern development as a commercial and industrial center resulted in the creation of a rather grimly practical urban environment. The image of Osaka as a treeless, gray wasteland persists in spite of several decades of efforts to improve the city's image. Several of the older urban parks—Nakanoshima, Hamadera, Tennō-ji, Sumiyoshi, and Osaka-jō—have been discussed in other chapters. The greening of Osaka has proceeded at an impressive rate, from the gingko trees along Midōsuji Street to the waterfowl sanctuary at Nankō (see page 117). The efforts have resulted in the creation of many new public parks, three of which are particularly interesting.

One of the largest and most intensively developed urban parks in Osaka is Hattori Ryokuchi Kōen. The park is in the northern suburb of Toyonaka; from the Midōsuji Line's Ryokuchi Kōen Station, a broad pedestrian street leads west directly into the park.

Ryokuchi Kōen, as it is generally called, features a variety of distinct areas and activities, rather loosely integrated by a system of landscaped paths. Although conceived primarily as a "green zone" according to the park's literature, it was clearly designed to provide something for everyone. As a result, the park lacks a strong overall identity, even though many of the individual sections are quite attractive.

At the main park entrance is a large European-style plaza, complete with a monumental fountain and geometrical paving designs. Unlike the spaces it was modeled on, however, the plaza is not an integral part of an urban district. Fortunately the park's visitors have supplied plenty of activities, if not the sort usually found in European plazas. Given the paucity of paved open space in Japanese cities, do not be surprised to find the plaza filled with young people playing catch and hitting tennis balls, and younger ones on bicycles, tricycles, or in strollers.

Other areas in the park include a formal flower garden, athletic fields, two boating ponds (lined with the ubiquitous anglers nonchalantly ignoring the equally ubiquitous "no fishing" signs), and two playgrounds whose scale and equipment strike the preschool set as humongous. The Japanese landscape garden is disappointing, due to both uninspired design and halfhearted maintenance. The park even contains an equestrian school for those who harbor fantasies of life as landed English aristocracy. An amphitheater and a rehearsal hall for the Osaka Philharmonic Orchestra opened in 1991. The music complex was designed by the Prefectural Building Department, which has developed an architectural design staff of high quality in recent years.

The best features of the park are its large, relatively natural green spaces, its botanical garden, and an open-air museum of Japanese traditional farmhouses (*minka*).

The green spaces include a large bamboo grove on a hillside, which provides a beautiful pale green focus for the park and a landmark for the surrounding neighborhood year-round. The bamboo grove is surrounded and crossed by winding paths favored by joggers. Much of the remainder of the park is landscaped in a lush and fairly naturalistic manner. There are also the mandatory cherry and plum groves, filled with picnickers during the *hanami* (flower-viewing) season in the spring. At this time of year, the trampled ground under the trees and the trash cans overflowing with the remains of hundreds of bento (box lunches) are proof of the park's popularity.

The botanical garden is separated from the main body of the park, but is well worth the effort to visit. In fact, its relative isolation may be at least partly responsible for its quiet atmosphere. The garden is entered through a handsome conservatory designed by local architect Taki Mitsuo, who has made a reputation as a designer of structures for parks and nature centers. The building contains a lush collection of tropical and semitropical plants, streams, and a sculptural waterfall. Beyond is a nicely landscaped garden suitable for strolling and providing an opportunity to learn the Japanese names for some familiar and exotic plants.

The open-air museum of Japanese farmhouses is the park's centerpiece. A total of eleven structures—seven houses and four related rural structures—have been brought together and reconstructed in the park. The farmhouses represent several styles and regions. The most popular of the buildings is a *gasshō-zukuri* house, a large structure with a tall, steeply pitched thatched roof. My personal favorite is a much more modest house from Nose, at the north end of Osaka Prefecture. The hipped and gabled roof of this building extends very low to the ground, making the house seem a part of the earth, while the internal arrangement of rooms is a model of simplicity and clarity. Throughout the museum, the dirt-floored utility spaces in the houses are open to the public, and in two or three of the houses you can remove your shoes and wander freely through the interiors. The setting is pleasantly landscaped in rural style, though the juxtaposition of houses from different regions, removed from their agricultural surroundings, is hardly realistic.

Although its popularity can sometimes render this green space a little too urban for comfort, the park's special events and activities make it more than just a place to relax under the trees. In spring and fall, stalls are set up by plant vendors, so that home gardeners or mere wishful thinkers can check out everything from vegetable seeds to bonsai. On weekends throughout the warm months *yaki-soba* (fried noodles), *okonomiyaki* (spicy pancakes), and the like can be bought from pushcarts at several locations around the park. The atmosphere of spontaneous recreation may even move you to join a few dozen others in an attempt to navigate a rowboat around a pond, to amuse the ducks and irritate the fishermen.

Further north, in Suita, is the even larger Banpaku Kinen Kōen (Expo Commemorative Park), which began as the site of Osaka's World Exposition of 1970. In the twenty years which have elapsed since that event, the park has evolved and matured into an exciting and surprising landscape, as well as a home to three excellent museums. Access to the park is via the Osaka Monorail, which now runs between Senri Chūō and Ibaraki, but is currently being extended.

The park is visible from a distance, thanks to architect Kikutake Kiyonori's steel tower studded with geodesic domes, originally part of Expo '70. Expo's huge surrealistic theme sculpture, "Tower of the Sun," also remains. Architects and urban planners consider Expo '70 a last gasp of the optimistic modernism that drove design and development in the postwar years. In light of today's more sober awareness of the limits of technological and architectural solutions to societal problems, it is perhaps fitting that Kikutake's tower is now closed and awaiting major repairs or even demolition.

Because the site was laid out to accommodate Expo buildings and crowds, the design was executed in broad strokes. When Expo '70 ended, and most of its pavilions were removed, additional plantings and other modifications were made in order to bring the park down to a cozier scale without obliterating the monumental outline of the original scheme. Many of the landscaping features are delightful, especially those created of stone and water. Some have that quality of artful naturalism belonging to the Japanese garden tradition, while others are determinedly modern in their abstract geometries. Rocky springs, promenades along rippling watercourses, ponds, and lakes form a network through the park. There is a spring that is a special favorite of children, who scramble over its jumble of boulders, while a large pool near the park's center has become a spot for the sailing and racing of beautifully crafted radio-controlled sailboats on weekends.

Expo Park contains a landscape garden which I believe is among the finest of the large modern Japanese-style gardens. It is one of a few which successfully fuse traditional elements with aspects of modern abstract design on the scale of a daimyo stroll garden. The grandeur of the scale is expressed in broad sweeping vistas and a generally expansive layout that immediately distinguish it from gardens of the past. When I first visited some fifteen years ago it seemed too open, but the plantings have matured along with my appreciation of the design. From the pavilion just inside the garden entrance, the view across a pond is especially fine. The trompe l'oeil hillside is a backdrop that appears much larger than its true size—as becomes evident when the occasional thoughtless visitor tramps across its summit like King Kong crossing Mt. Fuji.

The garden also showcases the full range of traditional flowering plants, with magnificent displays of blossoms throughout the growing season. The lotus pond is especially beautiful at its mid-June peak. Perhaps the best floral performance in the garden is put on by its azaleas during the month of May. A path between two low hills is lined with masses of azaleas which have themselves been pruned to form abstract hillsides of foliage and blossom. The seasonal changes which are a vital part of the Japanese garden tradition are given full expression here to wonderful effect.

Across from the garden entrance is the Osaka National Museum of Art, designed by Kawasaki Kiyoshi, one of the few buildings remaining from Expo '70. It is a fine exercise in the mode of late modern architecture that showcases exposed steel framing and large expanses of glass. Its simple wedge shape with louvered glass on the sloping roof provides a clean, well-lit environment for the display of the museum's collection, which consists of modern art, both Japanese and Western. The upper-level galleries are used for temporary exhibitions of many types, including large shows such as the exhibition a few years ago of ancient Near Eastern art from the British Museum.

The Japan Folk Crafts Museum next door makes a nice contrast. More modest in scale, the collection it houses is similarly restrained, and includes baskets, textiles, dolls, furniture, and pottery. Modern pieces created in the style or spirit of traditional crafts are exhibited along with older folk arts. A huge mural by Munakata Shikō, the late master of the modern woodblock print, is permanently displayed in the third gallery, while other items on exhibit are frequently changed.

The third museum in Expo Park is the National Museum of Ethnology, designed by Kurokawa Kishō in 1977. The museum is a masterful combination of high tech and high drama. Charcoal-gray surfaces are set off by details in stainless steel, aluminum, and brass. Behind a monumental stair leading to the galleries is a fascinating courtyard consisting of a series of stairs and platforms paved in tan stone. Completely cut off from public access, this space has a marvelous esoteric quality, as if created for the purpose of some as yet undiscovered ritual. On the floor above, stainless steel information capsules allow visitors to select educational videos from the museum's library. In the galleries, displays are dramatically spot-lit against dark backgrounds. In places the galleries are overcrowded, but a series of courtyards open to the sky provides relief.

The newest addition to the park's facilities is the International Institute for Children's Literature, a children's library that also hosts seminars and other events. If you are in Osaka with children you may be happy to learn that there are many English-language books, from picture books to juvenile fiction, available for borrowing.

PARKS

My only serious quarrel with the design of Expo Park has to do with its pedestrian network and the complicated system of admission tickets and receipts. For reasons that doubtless make sense from some organizational point of view, the area containing the museums and Japanese garden has been separated from the rest of the park by means of a tall and obtrusively ugly fence. Besides marring the views, the restricted access to the museum area creates a bottleneck at the single, makeshift entrance, and prevents visitors from walking in a natural and rational circuit along the northern edge of the park. The separation also restricts the north entrance and its associated street to taxis only. Adding to the frustration is the fact that this peculiar arrangement is not indicated on maps handed out at the park entrance, leaving you to discover the various abrupt dead ends for yourself. When passing from one section to another, you must remember to locate ticket-dispensing machines which allow you to return without paying an additional charge. Also, your general park admission ticket stub must be presented at the Japanese garden in order to receive a discount on the garden's admission fee.

Adjacent to the park is Expoland, a large but ordinary amusement park. Fortunately, Expo Park contains enough features to interest and exhaust even my seven-year-old son, so that we have managed to avoid Expoland on several trips to the park.

Returning to the city limits, there is another park whose origins are similar to those of the Expo '70 site. Tsurumi Ryokuchi Kōen began as the site of the International Flower and Greenery Exposition of 1990. Since the exposition ended, the park has been closed for the removal of temporary pavilions and reconstruction as a public park. A small section of the park reopened in April 1991; the renovation is not scheduled to be complete until 1997.

Reaching the park by public transportation is an experience in itself. The Tsurumi Ryokuchi subway line, built for the exposition, features spiffy new "linear motor cars." The linear motor is an old but formerly impractical type of electric motor which is now finding an application in rail transit. Leaving the technical details aside, the result is the smoothest and quietest subway ride ever (so smooth and quiet that one guidebook to Japan mistakenly described it as a "magnetic levitation" train line). In addition to a comfortable ride, the line features flashy electronic graphics, New Age musical arrival and departure themes, and stations designed in whimsical postmodern style. This short subway line runs from Kyōbashi for only five stops to Tsurumi Ryokuchi Station.

Judging by the portion of the park visible now, its style will be considerably different from that of the Expo '70 park. Rather than space-age towers, the principal landmarks here are a Dutch windmill reproduction and what appears to be an oversized and brightly colored Sumerian column with a restaurant on top. An aura of futurism is still present, but cloaked in eclectic if not downright frivolous garb. Different though it is in style, the park is being developed as a showpiece for the city, so there is hope that it may eventually be a match for Expo Park in quality.

HATTORI RYOKUCHI KŌEN   Admissions: Botanical Garden, ¥200; Farmhouse Museum (tel. 06-862-3137), ¥410.

BANPAKU KINEN KŌEN   Admissions: Expo Park ¥100; Landscape Garden (tel. 06-877-1039), ¥200; Osaka National Museum of Art (tel. 06-876-2481), ¥350; Japan Folk Crafts Museum (tel. 06-877-1971), ¥350; National Museum of Ethnology (tel. 06-876-2151), ¥350; Expoland (tel. 06-877-0560), ¥600; other areas, no additional charge. Expo Park attractions open at 9-10 A.M. and close at 4-4:30 P.M. All are closed Wednesdays.

INTERNATIONAL INSTITUTE OF CHILDREN'S LITERATURE   (located within Expo Park) 9:30 A.M. to 5 P.M. Closed Wednesdays and from December 28 to January 4.

TSURUMI RYOKUCHI KŌEN   11 A.M. to 5 P.M. (tel. 06-912-0650). Closed Mondays and days following national holidays.

ESCAPING THE CITY

It can sometimes seem that the city of Osaka is endless, that the network of train lines, street grids, and shopping arcades continues indefinitely to the horizon in all directions. The city's underground passages and shopping districts also enhance the feeling, the Umeda underground sometimes becoming a Kafkaesque, directionless maze. Yet the boundaries of the city are remarkably well defined and close at hand, if not often visible through the smog. Along these edges—mountains in three directions, Osaka Bay in the fourth—escape from the city can be swift and satisfying.

Three of my favorite places of refuge are presented below. All are within Osaka Prefecture and are easily accessible when urban stresses demand immediate relief. The principal feature of all three is that there are few people and a great deal of open space, but each has its special attractions, cultural as well as natural.

Fumin no Mori (Prefectural Citizens' Forest) consists of eight patches of wooded mountainside along the eastern edge of the prefecture, totalling about 543 hectares. All eight areas are contained within the much larger (15,620 hectares) Kongō-Ikoma Quasi-National Park, which straddles the border between Osaka and Nara prefectures. Most of Fumin no Mori consists of hiking trails, which often extend into adjacent sections of Kongō-Ikoma, but campgrounds and other recreational areas are also present.

The largest (142 hectares) and most easily accessible area in Fumin no Mori is called the Narukawa Enchi. It can be reached from Hiraoka Station on the Kintetsu Nara Line in 30 minutes by local train from Namba. (A less strenuous approach is to begin at the top of Mt. Ikoma by taking the cable car up from Ikoma Station, an express stop on the Kintetsu Nara Line. This route has the disadvantage of leading past an amusement park and a series of television and microwave antennas before reaching the hiking trails.)

From Hiraoka Station, the entrance to Hiraoka Jinja is clearly visible, and makes an excellent starting point for cleansing the mind of urban grime. The shrine has a venerable history; it is a Kasuga shrine, said to be the ancestor of the more famous Kasuga Taisha in Nara. However, the main compound has been newly reconstructed, and the fresh scent and warm glow of recently finished lumber, as well as the intense crimson paint of the innermost buildings create an impression much different than the aged patina we often associate with Shinto shrines. With the mountain as a backdrop, and several ancient trees preserved within the shrine precinct, these fresh, pristine buildings beautifully express the Shinto values of cleanliness and purity. From the shrine entrance, several paths lead up through Hiraoka Park to Fumin no Mori. A few signs in English are found throughout the area, though most are in Japanese only. However, given the nature of the terrain, it would be difficult to go seriously astray. The condition of the trails varies greatly, from pristine to ankle-deep in mud. All the trails are steep, so after a relatively short ascent Osaka appears far below. The main trail follows a ridge, providing frequent and sometimes spectacular views, while valley trails feature the more intimate pleasures of rushing water, birdcalls, and an occasional small Buddhist temple punctuating the landscape.

At higher elevations signs of human visitors become fewer. Along secondary trails which branch off from the main routes, you may spook a covey of quail or a sunning skink. Of course, this is not primal forest. Outside the Hiraoka shrine precinct, ancient trees are not to be found. The mountainside has been a source of lumber and fuel for generations of local residents. Fortunately, however, no large areas appear to have been clear-cut in modern times. Clear-cut forests are generally replanted almost exclusively in a single species of conifer, but Fumin no Mori features a mix of deciduous trees with broadleaf evergreens and a few conifers. While the distribution of species and the relatively small sizes of the trees are the result of human activities, the general mix is characteristic of native vegetation for a Japanese temperate forest.

Reaching the ridge which forms the western edge of Narukawa Enchi, and of Osaka Prefecture, requires at least a 90-minute hike. From there the summit of Mt. Ikoma is a short distance to the north, while the bulk of the Kongō-Ikoma Park stretches out to the south. Maps are available, in Japanese only, at an office near the top of the main trail in the Narukawa Enchi, or in Osaka at the Prefectural Greening Office, Chūō-ku, Honmachi 1-4-8, second floor.

Mountain scenery of a different sort can be found at Meiji no Mori Minoo Quasi-National Park. Although it received the national park designation in 1968, the Minoo River gorge and waterfall have been well known as a scenic area for at least two hundred years. Since the middle of the Tokugawa period, artists and intellectuals have journeyed to the Minoo gorge to paint, compose poetry, and especially to celebrate the beauty of the maple leaves in autumn.

Minoo is at the end of a branch of the Hankyu Railway, about 35 minutes from Umeda. The main route to the gorge and waterfall is unmistakable, as souvenir shops give way to inns along the approach. The atmosphere is of a rather old-fashioned, low-key resort town. It is a gentle stroll up the valley toward the waterfall along a paved path lined with maples. Though most spectacular in the autumn, the soft shade under their pale green canopy is also delightful on a hot summer day. Along the road is Ryūan-ji, a Tendai sect temple said to have been founded in the seventh century. Extant buildings date from the Tokugawa period and thereafter.

The main route through the park is marred by developments intended, no doubt, for the safety and convenience of visitors. Ramshackle restaurants and obtrusive concrete shelters crop up virtually at the foot of the waterfall, and large expanses of chain-link netting cover many of the steep slopes flanking the river, obscuring the craggy, moss-covered rocks.

Above the falls is a highway and parking lot. This area seems to be the favorite hangout of a local monkey population which apparently subsists on handouts from park visitors. The monkeys are cute and somewhat tame, but they are extremely protective of their food, and seem especially agressive toward children who venture too close.

Minoo Park also offers more isolated hiking trails. A visitors' center is located about 1 kilometer up the highway from the falls. The center contains displays of local history, flora and fauna, and an excellent scale model of the park area. Maps of hiking trails are also available. All of the displays and maps are in Japanese, though the maps have major destinations labeled in English.

The best of the many hiking trails in the area is Tōkai Shizen Hodō (Tōkai Nature Trail), which begins near the visitors' center and continues as far as Tokyo Prefecture. The Meiji no Mori Takao Quasi-National Park at the eastern end of the trail was, like Minoo Park, established in 1968, in commemoration of the hundredth anniversary of the Meiji Restoration. The section of the trail that is in Minoo Park is used by relatively serious and considerate hikers. As a result, the trail is in excellent condition and remarkably free of the litter which detracts from the scenery in most Japanese parks, including the lower reaches of Minoo. A hike of a little under an hour will take you to the trail's highest elevation, where there is a splendid view of Osaka city and harbor on a clear day.

A few hundred meters further along, a small, steep trail branches off to the right. At the end of a rather harrowing downhill scramble, the trail ends at Katsuo-ji. The buildings are not especially distinguished, but the setting is beautiful. As a traditional pilgrimage temple, Katsuo-ji has good facilities for visitors, including a restaurant near the main entrance gate. And if the return hike seems too daunting, there is infrequent bus service from Katsuo-ji to Kita Senri and Senri Chūō stations.

While Minoo Park has a long history as a natural retreat, my last selection is a product of contemporary Japan in the most literal sense. On the reclaimed land of Nankō—along with high-rise housing blocks, container shipping facilities, and the INTEX exhibition hall complex—is the Nankō Yachō Kōen (Nankō Wild Bird Sanctuary).

A 40-minute ride from Umeda on the Yotsubashi Line and the New Tram takes you to Nakafutō. There is an inconspicuous shelter near the entrance path to INTEX, where you can borrow a bicycle (for free!) to pedal to the bird sanctuary. The waterfront promenade has been attractively developed, so you may prefer to walk the 2 kilometers instead. The route is also wheelchair accessible, as is the main pavilion of the bird sanctuary. The most pleasant surprise of all is that there is not a single souvenir stand or restaurant to be found along the full length of the promenade.

At the center of the sanctuary is a large pavilion (admission is also free), which has a continuous strip of windows overlooking three shallow ponds. Two are filled with fresh water, the third with sea water. Typical shoreline plants surround the ponds. Waterfowl and shore birds are abundant year round, with migratory species making seasonal appearances. Displays in the pavilion give English, Japanese, and scientific names for many species. On a quiet day (which seems to be the norm), the manager may even loan you a spotting scope on a short tripod.

Walking paths in the sanctuary are densely landscaped. The plantings have not been pruned in the mannered style generally found in Japanese parks. Instead, they have been selected and maintained with an eye to providing screening, cover, and food for the bird population. At each end of the park is a blind with sliding metal shutters, providing additional vantage points for birdwatching.

This is not a location likely to attract serious birdwatchers hoping to add species to their life lists. Nor is it likely to satisfy hyperactive children in school groups. Ironically, it is the lack of attractions which makes the bird sanctuary attractive—if you crave the solitary, serene enjoyment of birds flying, diving, and calling, accompanied by the slow and stately procession of ships in the harbor beyond.

Of course, if you are living in Osaka, none of these places is an adequate substitute for a week's vacation. But when time or money, or both, are in short supply, these quick escapes from the city can be had for the cost of a train ticket and half a day. A modest price when your sanity is on the line.

NANKŌ YACHŌ KŌEN   9 A.M. to 5 P.M. Closed Wednesdays (tel. 06-613-5556).

MINOO PARK VISITOR'S CENTER   (tel. 0727-23-0649).

DINING
SHOPPING
AND MORE

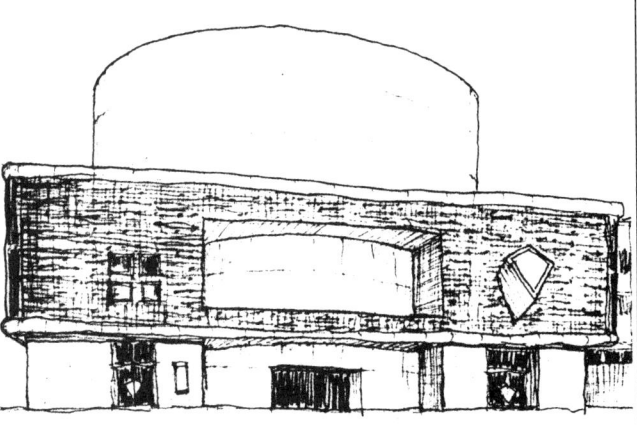

SOURCES OF INFORMATION

OSAKA TOURIST INFORMATION CENTERS Sponsored by the city, these centers are good first stops on your way into Osaka. They offer various brochures and a free map, and have English-speaking staff. The map is overly simplified, as is the accompanying rail route map, but adequate to at least get you oriented. The centers are located in Shin-Osaka Station on the third floor (tel. 06-305-3311) and in Osaka Station at the east entrance (tel. 06-345-2189).

OSAKA INTERNATIONAL HOUSE This organization, supported by both private and public sponsors, opened its headquarters in 1987 at 8-2-6 Uehommachi, Tennōji-ku (tel. 06-772-5931). The facility includes hotel rooms, a conference center, and an information center and library. International House has published a comprehensive English guide to Osaka, entitled *Catch Osaka*, available only at its headquarters. The guide is especially useful for foreign residents, as it lists medical facilities and includes how-to information on the post office, shopping, and driving, among other useful topics. As a guidebook, *Catch Osaka* is encyclopedic, but lacks an editorial viewpoint; the good, the bad, and the ugly are not distinguished in its descriptions. In addition, its proposed tours of the city's districts are based on an impossibly compressed time frame—each of its "one-day tours" would require most of a week to complete. The International House library is an excellent resource for travel information covering all of Japan, and contains a good selection of English-language books on other Japan-related topics as well. Its staff is helpful and knowledgable.

OSAKA FOUNDATION OF INTERNATIONAL EXCHANGE (OFIX) Like the Osaka International House, this group has a small English library on Japanese subjects, as well as a well-staffed information center. Their office is in the Osaka Business Park, Mid Tower (one of the Twin Tower group), fourteenth floor (tel. 06-945-6071). The map published by OFIX is the best of

SOURCES OF INFORMATION

the free maps in English, and the only one I found which covers the entire prefecture.

KANSAI TIME OUT   This English-language monthly magazine is an excellent source of information on services and activities in the Kansai region, which includes Osaka, Kobe, and Kyoto. Advertisers include restaurants, real estate agents, travel agents, non-profit organizations, and just about anyone else desiring to make contact with the local foreign community. The magazine is available at major bookstores or through their offices at SU Press, 1-13 Ikuta-chō 1-chōme, Chūō-ku, Kobe 651 (tel. 078-232-4516).

DINING

Osaka's reputation as a gourmet center is centuries-old and well deserved. The city's nickname "the kitchen of Japan" refers to the warehouses and markets for rice, fish, and vegetables that developed out of its unique economic·status during the Momoyama and Edo periods; the phrase *kuidaore*, meaning roughly "bankrupted by indulgence in food," gives you a better idea of the importance of dining to the traditional culture of Osaka.

The multitude of restaurants and bars in Osaka makes any listing quite arbitrary. A few choices, such as Kitchō and Kani Dōraku, will appear in most guidebook selections. The rest I've chosen for any of several reasons—quality of food, convenience of location, high value for low cost, local color or otherwise intriguing atmosphere, or simply because my memory of an enjoyable evening spent there has colored my view of its worth.

For those new to travel in Japan, it is worth knowing that a variety of small restaurants can be found on the top floor of any major department store. These are generally moderate in price and quality. I have not listed any of the ubiquitous and nondescript eateries found in the vicinity of every train and subway station in the prefecture, and you won't have to search far for a McDonald's or a Kentucky Fried Chicken (KFC).

UMEDA AND VICINITY

HANKYU SANBANGAI COMPLEX The lowest level of this underground shopping mall contains dozens of restaurants, generally a cut above the typical selection in both quality and price. Among the Sanbangai restaurants, some favorites are Botejyū, an *okonomiyaki* chain (these spicy pancakes are an Osaka specialty); Raja, for curried rice; Fukamoto, for tempura; Kazoku-tei, for soba and udon noodles; and Aka-hyōtan, for salads.

ISARIBI The contrast with the squeaky-clean Sanbangai Complex could hardly be greater. Isaribi is a *robata-yaki* (literally, "grilled on the hearth") restaurant, in which customers sit at a bar with a large grill in the center. Dishes are ordered individually from a menu or by simply pointing at the ingredients spread out beside the grill, and prepared as you watch. It's possible to eat cheaply here, though the temptation to sample yet another dish (at ¥300 each) is strong. Local color it has in abundance, with the atmosphere of a friendly dive. It is difficult to find, in the basement of a building near the northwest corner of the Sanbangai—see map 1 for this and the other Umeda restaurants listed below.

HONJIN This bar is one among many in the shopping and entertainment district of Sonezaki, south and east of Osaka Station. Sonezaki is popular with local office workers; hence it is as crowded on weeknights as on weekends. Honjin is distinguished by its wide selection of brands of sakè from around Japan; look for the illuminated map of Japan on its signboard.

ICHIRIKI With good sushi at exceptionally low prices, Ichiriki is an office workers' favorite in Sonezaki.

HIDEYOSHI Another *robata-yaki* restaurant, Hideyoshi's dishes are cheaper and in smaller portions than at Isaribi; it's also easier to find.

CENTRAL OSAKA

KITCHŌ This is the restaurant frequented by prime ministers, captains of industry, and their VIP guests. It is a *kaiseki* restaurant, meaning that a dozen or more small courses are served in succession, each presented in the most elegant and visually pleasing manner imaginable. One memorable course consisted of daikon radishes carved in the shape of lanterns and lit from within by candles; the lanterns were surrounded by slices of raw fish. Reservations are required, and prices are astronomical—around ¥40,000 per person. Chūō-ku, Kōrai-bashi 2-6-7 (tel. 06-231-1937). Note: There are now Kitchō branches, including one in the Royal Hotel, which serve a toned-down version of the original's creations at a modest ¥10,000 per meal.

TAIKŌ-EN   Primarily a wedding and banquet center, and featuring several dining rooms serving different styles of Japanese and Western food, Taikō-en is located on the former Fujita estate near Kyōbashi Station, just across the street from the Fujita Museum (see map 2). Banquet rooms and private dining rooms are located in prewar remnants of the estate; the new dining rooms also provide views of the fine landscape garden. Reservations are strongly recommended. Miyakojima-ku, Amijima-chō 9-10 (tel. 06-356-1111).

D/A BRASSERIE   Just northwest of the plaza in front of the Keihan Kyōbashi Station is a striking contemporary building with a concave, mirrored facade, designed by Shinohara Kazuo and called K2. An entrance to the basement level, around the back of the building, leads to D/A, a fashionable bar decorated in a startling, decadent, dark-humored, high-tech style. Drinks are a bit pricey, but the atmosphere is worth it. Dōjima-ku, Higashi Notamachi 2-9 (tel. 06-351-9173).

COUNTRY LIFE   This restaurant offers a vegetarian buffet with both Japanese and Western dishes (it's operated by foreigners). Prices are moderate, the food wholesome and tasty (if you still think of tofu as something alien, its time to shake off the ethnocentrism and enjoy one of Japan's premier foods). Located about two blocks west of Temmabashi Station on the south side of Tosabori-dōri (see map 2). Chūō-ku, Kitahama Higashi 2-13 (tel. 06-943-9597).

SHINSAIBASHI AND NAMBA
For directions, refer to map 3.

NISHIKE   The specialty here is *udon* noodles, one of the foods for which Osaka is known. The *udon-chiri*, a deluxe cooked-at-the-table version, is recommended.

SHIRUKIYO   This small, folksy restaurant serves *oden*, another Osaka specialty, and *teishoku*, set meals which include rice, soup, pickles, and a

DINING

small main dish. Nice atmosphere, with all seating at a single counter, Shirukiyo is popular for drinking and light meals.

MARUMAN HONKE Established in 1864, but now in modern quarters, Maruman serves *uo-suki*, a local version of sukiyaki which substitutes fish for beef.

PIG AND WHISTLE A popular hangout for foreigners, this classic pub is located in the expatriot haven of Shinsaibashi and is open after 4 P.M. IS building, Chūō-ku, Shinsaibashi-suji 2-1-32.

KANI DŌRAKU The famous mechanical crab marks the original Kani Dōraku (there are now branches in several cities). The crab dishes are good, but the tourist-trap atmosphere is hard to ignore, as is the location, at the intersection of the Shinsaibashi-suji arcade and Dōtombori.

MOTI A good Indian restaurant located two doors east and three floors up from Kani Dōraku, Moti's prices are moderate.

Adjacent to Hōzen-ji in the Namba area is a network of narrow pedestrian streets called Hōzen-ji Yokochō, home of several fine restaurants, including the four noted here.

SUMO CHAYA The specialty here is *chanko-nabe*, the staple dish of sumo wrestlers. It is not a high-starch and animal-fat concoction such as American football players favor, but a tasty combination of fish, chicken, vegetables, and noodles cooked at your table in a rich, citrus-flavored broth.

SHŌBENTANGO-TEI This is a drinking and eating establishment whose down-home atmosphere is suggested by the name—*shōben tango* is a bucket that served farmers as a chamberpot in the days before indoor plumbing.

TAKOUME The name means "Octopus Plum," and it specializes in the former, along with seafood of all species. Like Shōbentango-tei, it's another unpretentious "old Osaka" restaurant mentioned in Oda Sakunosuke's stories.

AJI-BIL The Aji Building is a collection of restaurants housed in a building designed by Ishii Osamu, one of Osaka's finest contemporary architects. The *mingei* (folk art) feeling of the first-floor restaurant is especially pleasing.

HOTELS, INNS, AND HOSTELS

I make no claim to expert knowledge of Osaka's hotels. The selection which follows is intended to provide accommodations in a variety of price ranges and locations. The list is organized in a roughly geographical fashion, north to south.

SENRI TO SHIN-OSAKA

HATTORI YOUTH HOSTEL   1-13 Hattori Ryokuchi, Toyonaka (tel. 06-699-5631). This hostel is located in Hattori Ryokuchi Kōen (see page 107), a 15-minute walk from the Ryokuchi Kōen Station on the Midōsuji subway line. The most economical choice available, its rooms are dormitory style (six guests per room), with a bath down the hall.

OSAKA CORONA HOTEL   1-3-21 Nishi Awaji, Higashi Yodogawa-ku (tel. 06-323-3151). This modest and reasonably priced business hotel is a few minutes' walk northeast of Shin-Osaka Station (leave the station by the east gate's north exit). The hotel is visible to your right, a brick-red stucco building.

NEW OSAKA HOTEL   1-16-6 Higashi Nakajima, Higashi Yodogawa-ku (tel. 06-325-0011). The New Osaka also offers business-class accommodations, but it's a little more expensive than Osaka Corona, probably because the location is even more favorable relative to Shin-Osaka Station. It is clearly visible from the station's central exit.

SHIN-OSAKA WASHINGTON HOTEL   5-5-15 Nishi Nakajima, Yodogawa-ku (tel. 06-303-8111, fax 06-302-7007). Newer, flashier, and slightly higher than the New Osaka, the Washington Hotel also seems better able to deal with non-Japanese-speaking guests. Also visible from the station's central gate, it is a shiny white high-rise.

HOTELS, INNS, AND HOSTELS

UMEDA

OSAKA HILTON   1-8-8 Umeda, Kita-ku (tel. 06-347-7111). Umeda's most expensive hotel, the Hilton lives up to its reputation.

OSAKA TERMINAL HOTEL   3-1-1 Umeda, Kita-ku (tel. 06-344-1235). Only a small step down in price from the Hilton, all rooms are on Floors 21 to 26 and boast good views. The entrance is directly adjacent to the Osaka Station central concourse.

UMEDA OS HOTEL   2-11-5 Sonezaki, Kita-ku (tel. 06-312-1271). Umeda OS is a moderately priced business hotel convenient to Umeda's transportation and entertainment center. It is located a few doors south of Asahiya bookstore on Midōsuji Street.

CENTRAL OSAKA

HOTEL NEW OTANI OSAKA   1-4-1 Shiromi, Chūō-ku (tel. 06-941-1111). Like all the hotels in this chain, it is luxurious and expensive. Its location in the Osaka Business Park is convenient for castle visitors as well as high-powered business people.

OSAKA CASTLE HOTEL   1-1 Temmabashi Kyōmachi, Chūō-ku (tel. 06-942-2401). Still expensive at half the Otani's rate, the Castle Hotel is ideally located for subways (Temmabashi Station), the castle, and Nakanoshima's east end.

ROYAL HOTEL   5-3-68 Nakanoshima, Kita-ku (tel. 06-448-1121). This luxury hotel gathers and disseminates information about attractions and events in Osaka and the Kansai region. Its restaurants include a branch of Kitchō (see page 124). The Royal is surprisingly distant from public transportation given its central location.

HOTELS, INNS, AND HOSTELS

SHINSAIBASHI AND NAMBA

HOTEL NIKKO OSAKA   1-3-3 Nishi Shinsaibashi, Chūō-ku (tel. 06-244-1111, fax 06-245-2432). This luxury hotel in Shinsaibashi is accessible directly from the subway station (Exit 8). It features a non-smoking floor and a floor of suites decorated by fashion designer Hanae Mori.

HOLIDAY INN NANKAI-OSAKA   15-5-2 Shinsaibashi-suji, Chūō-ku (tel. 06-213-8281, fax 06-213-8640). The Holiday Inn is several blocks north of Namba subway station on Midōsuji Street. It's less expensive than the Nikko, and has a rooftop swimming pool.

BUSINESS HOTEL OHTANI   2-8-22 Nishi Shinsaibashi, Chūō-ku (tel. 06-211-1124). This business hotel is two blocks west of Midōsuji Street in Shinsaibashi.

IMPERIAL HOTEL (TEIKOKU HOTERU)   2-8-17 Nishi Shinsaibashi, Chūō-ku (tel. 06-211-8151). The Imperial is another business hotel in Shinsaibashi, just south of the Ohtani.

D-HOTEL   2-5-15 Dōtombori, Chūō-ku (tel. 06-212-2995, fax 06-212-7462). The hotel for lovers of contemporary architecture, D-Hotel was designed by Takeyama Sei, a rising star of the Japanese design world, and opened in 1990. Rooms are stylishly austere, not at all the overstuffed approach found in most medium- to high-priced hotels. D-Hotel is readily identified as an eight-story convex-walled wedge of concrete at the west end of the Dōtombori arcade. It's a small hotel, so reserve rooms well in advance.

CAPSULE HOTEL ASAHI PLAZA SHINSAIBASHI   2-12-22 Nishi Shinsaibashi, Chūō-ku (tel. 06-213-1991). Osaka is the home of the original capsule hotel, in which business people who party too late to catch the last train home can sleep in a beehive-like environment, for roughly half the cost

HOTELS, INNS, AND HOSTELS

of a business-class hotel room. If you want to experience the "real Japan," this capsule hotel is a spiffy new example of the type, two blocks west of Midōsuji Street.

EBISU-SŌ RYOKAN   1-7-33 Nipponbashi-nishi, Chūō-ku (tel. 06-643-4861). This is a ryokan (Japanese inn) in the sense that rooms are Japanese style, and the bath is shared by all guests, but it doesn't have the service, meals, or high cost of more traditional Japanese-style inns. For about the cost of a capsule hotel, you have your own room rather than a crawl-in cell. The checkout time of 10 A.M. is strictly enforced. From the south end of the Nankai City complex in Namba, head east one block, then south about four blocks to the T-shaped intersection; the Ebisu-sō is straight ahead.

SOUTHERN OSAKA PREFECTURE

KAWACHI NAGANO YOUTH HOSTEL   1305-2 Amano-chō, Kawachi Nagano (tel. 0721-53-1010). This hostel offers simple accommodations in the heart of the beautiful Kawachi Nagano area, and is located just south of Kongō-ji at the Kansai Cycle Center bus stop.

BOOKSTORES AND SPECIALTY SHOPPING

Osaka is a shopper's paradise; when it comes to contemporary consumer products, the opportunities are numbingly abundant. What may go unnoticed in the deluge of designer fashions and teeny little electronic devices are the specialty shops and districts catering to more limited audiences.

One such category of shops is bookstores. Osaka has a long and proud heritage as a center of publishing and as home to many fine writers and other literary figures. For a time during the Tokugawa period, Osaka had as many as 564 publishing companies, more than any other Japanese city. This flourishing of literary activity was the result both of Osaka's economic power and the relatively lax attitude of the Tokugawa regime toward its governance. Writers flourished along with the publishing industry; the playwright Chikamatsu Monzaemon, novelist Ihara Saikaku, and poet/painter Yosa Buson were all Osaka natives. A disproportionate number of modern Japan's novelists and poets hail from Osaka, including Kawabata Yasunari and Oda Sakunosuke. Tanizaki Jun'ichirō adopted Osaka as his home after the Great Kanto Earthquake devastated Tokyo in 1923. Although superceded by Tokyo both as a publishing and bookselling center, Osaka can still satisfy the needs of both the scholar and the casual reader.

If you are a foreign resident in Japan, bookstores that carry titles in your native tongue are essential for maintaining a semblance of emotional stability. In Osaka, the best-known bookstore among English-speakers is Kinokuniya, located at the foot of the main entrance to the Hankyu Umeda Station. Kinokuniya is a vast, one-story shop, and probably carries more English titles than any other bookstore in the city. The subject matter is impressively varied, including literature, both popular and classical; books about Japan and the Japanese language; business-related titles; children's books; imported magazines; and even self-help and pop philosophy books.

Kinokuniya's popularity is also its main problem. Although the store is reasonably well organized and the aisles fairly wide, shopping at Kinokuniya is always a mob scene, less than enjoyable for those not acclimated to

Japanese densities. Sundays and lunch hours are particularly intense: you have been warned.

To avoid the crowds, you need only venture briefly outside Umeda's endless underground mall. Standing at the south end of the Hankyu "cathedral" (so called because of its pseudo-Gothic vaulted ceiling and stained-glass windows), you can see the red and white sign for the Asahiya bookstore on the left side of Midōsuji Street about a block to the south. You can also see no safe path to walk there; you will have to descend into the underground mall and cross under the street, then ascend again at the southeast corner of the intersection.

Asahiya may be less comprehensive than Kinokuniya, but still has an excellent selection of English titles. It is also a more pleasant place in which to browse. The store is five floors high, an arrangement that makes each level easy to navigate, even though Asahiya is nearly as busy as Kinokuniya. English titles are on the fifth floor.

The other major seller of current English-language books is a Maruzen branch at Temmabashi. Maruzen is in the Matsuzakaya department store at Temmabashi Station, on the top floor. It is considerably smaller and less popular than the two mentioned above, but has a good selection, including some books not available in the larger stores. It also has a reading area and an atmosphere generally conducive to enjoying rather than just shopping for books.

Osaka also has a good selection of secondhand bookstores. There is no Osaka equivalent of Kanda, the famous Tokyo book dealers' district. Instead, booksellers are dispersed around the city and into its suburbs.

The largest, oldest, and most comprehensive of the used-book dealers is the memorably named Tengyū ("heavenly cow"), which is the owner's unusual surname. Tengyū is a famous mecca for scholars, both Japanese and foreign. The store was formerly situated downtown, and was mentioned in a short story by Oda Sakunosuke set in the 1930s. Tengyū has recently moved to a stylish new concrete building in the northern suburbs. Take the Midōsuji subway line north to Ryokuchi Kōen Station, then walk

BOOKSTORES AND SPECIALTY SHOPPING

south as far as the McDonald's (there's a McDonald's north of the station as well, so make sure of your orientation). Behind the golden arches is Tengyū's building, with the store occupying the first two of five floors.

The selection of art books is particularly strong, but there is an ample range of both scholarly and popular titles, antique block-printed first editions and slightly used comics. English-language paperbacks are available at low prices, but selection is hit-and-miss. Tengyū's new location is a rarity among secondhand bookstores—well lit, uncrowded, and comprehensibly organized.

Second to Tengyū as a booklover's hangout is Kosho-no-machi ("old book town") under the Hankyu tracks at street level just north of the Sanbangai complex in Umeda. Kosho-no-machi is a collection of a dozen or so small bookstores under a single roof. Each has its own specialties. At least one features foreign titles, mainly in two categories: books about Japan by foreign writers, ranging from naive nineteenth-century journals describing quaint and curious customs to a first edition of Ruth Benedict's *Chrysanthemum and the Sword*; and books on such popular arts as film and music. The stores which make up Kosho-no-machi maintain a high standard of quality, though some are so tightly packed with books that locating particular titles without the owner's assistance would appear hopeless and extracting them hazardous. Prices tend to be higher here than at Tengyū.

A seedier version of the "old book town" approach can be found in the former Osaka baseball stadium at Namba, immediately south of the Nankai Station and Namba City shopping complex. The sellers' stalls here are nearly all crammed to the ceiling with books. Much of the merchandise consists of *manga* (comic books) and soft-core pornography. Piles of comics tied in bundles, skin magazines in plastic wrappers, and racks of naughty video cassettes dominate the landscape. High up on inaccessible shelves "legitimate" titles and antique books can be seen here and there, but the experience is not unlike that of sorting through the garbage in search of lost jewelry.

The most peculiar of Osaka's used bookstores is located in Jūsō, on the Hankyu Rail Line. From the station's east exit, walk down the shopping arcade and turn left at the second intersection. Just ahead is a four-story, gray-tiled office building which contains the Academy Travel and Used Books office.

The bookselling operation there seems to have developed as a sideline to the travel agency; travelers need reading material, after all. The selection is predominantly English-language paperbacks, as the travel agency caters to foreign travelers. There is a mishmash of titles in other categories, from reference books to porn. That the business has developed haphazardly is evidenced by the lack of organization and space in the corner of the office given over to the books. There is a rough division into categories and an even rougher attempt at alphabetical organization within the categories, but misfiling is rampant. The aisles are too narrow for two people to pass. But if you want to stock up on escapist fiction for a long summer vacation without paying new book prices, Academy will probably have what you're after. They will also buy your old paperbacks (for a pittance) when your apartment or suitcase approaches critical mass.

If Osaka's secondhand and antiquarian book dealers are scattered about the city, its antique stores and art galleries have been increasingly concentrated in one area. In Nishi Temma-ku, between Umeda and Nakanoshima and east of Shin Midōsuji Street, a gallery district was formed in the 1960s and has continued to grow. The district is centered on a five- or six-block stretch of Oimatsu-dōri (also known as Garō-dōri, "gallery street"). Along this street and those that branch off from it are over thirty-five antique dealers and some thirty galleries of modern art.

Shops offer wares ranging from junk-store "collectibles" to Han-dynasty bronze mirrors. Some invite browsing, while the priciest keep their treasures hidden, bringing them out only at the customer's request. Osakans are known for their conservative taste; perhaps this is why even the modern art galleries show relatively little avant-garde work.

The other popular venues for antique collecting occur on festival days at Shitennō-ji and Sumiyoshi Taisha. These are real flea markets, complete with traditional fast-food stalls, fortunetellers, and an uneven assortment from cheap toys to used blue jeans to antiques of modest quality and sometimes questionable provenance. Enjoying the atmosphere of the event is

BOOKSTORES AND SPECIALTY SHOPPING

justification enough to visit these flea markets; the remote possibility of discovering some treasure is an added incentive. Shitennō-ji's markets are held on the twenty-first day of each month. Sumiyoshi's occur once every sixty days, on "Dragon Days" according to the old Chinese calendar.

A few other shopping districts are worth noting here because they convey a sense of the character of Osaka. The city's mercantile history and its reputation as a distribution center are still expressed in the specialized wholesale districts.

Of the many specialized wholesale districts around Osaka, the most fascinating is Dōguya-suji, the "kitchen utensil street" found two blocks due east of the Nankai Station at Namba. Dōguya-suji is an appropriate memorial to a city known in the Tokugawa period as "the kitchen of Japan." All the necessities can be found here in the way of Japanese restaurant supplies, from gas ranges to tableware to pot-bellied *tanuki* statues. The stores are all open to the public, though sales clerks used to dealing in quantity can sometimes be brusque toward indecisive foreigners trying to pick a single teapot. Like all the wholesale districts, product display is unaffectedly straightforward—row upon row of goods squeezed into the minimum of space—so don't move too quickly or carry too much baggage. The highlight of the street is undoubtedly the plastic model displays. You can send a friend a mug of Kirin, complete with a foamy head, or create your own eternally fresh salad from an array of tantalizing produce. The craftsmanship involved in the creation of these models is impressive, though the idea of expending one's talent in a career of painting ersatz yellowtail sashimi does seem a bit odd. Prices reflect the skill involved; I settled for a "light lunch" of sushi instead of the multi-course "meal" I would have liked.

Another unique shopping experience is to be found at the so-called International Market, located under the elevated tracks of the JR and Kintetsu railways at Tsuruhashi Station. This market originated in the postwar years as a black market outlet, and it retains a disreputable air in its dark maze of narrow alleys and shallow stalls. A trek through the warren-like market is like a journey to some other Japan, one somehow isolated from the sparkling glamour that the country's modern marketers so diligently pro-

BOOKSTORES AND SPECIALTY SHOPPING

mote. Shopping here has an almost primal character, a hunting-gathering expedition with ¥10,000 bills and Elephant Family shopping bags. The merchandise available runs the full gamut of shopping arcade goods, with some surprising specialties. There is an unusual number of stores selling leather products and fur coats, for example. The market also specializes in Korean products, especially lavishly embroidered and colored textiles. (Osaka has the largest Korean population in Japan.)

This has been a limited and highly biased view of specialty shopping in Osaka. As I noted at the outset, the range of possibilities is virtually endless. For the gourmet crowd, there is a fish and produce market street, Kuromon, just southeast of Nipponbashi Station, selling both wholesale and retail. Den-den Town, centered on Sakai-suji Street (a 5-minute walk east of the Nankai Namba Station) is the electronics district, with a stunning variety of gadgets, though the prices are not as heavily discounted as in Tokyo's famous Akihabara district. Five hundred meters east of Tanimachi 6-chōme Station is Matchamachi-suji, specializing in traditional dolls and toys. Traditional footwear can be found at Nipponbashi 3-chōme, and Tachibana-dōri, near Yotsubashi Station, is the furniture wholesale street.

MUSEUMS AND ASSORTED MONUMENTS

Osaka's museums are sufficiently numerous and diverse to provide satisfaction for all tastes. I have discussed many of them in previous chapters, but there are at least as many which are off the beaten path. Those discussed below are all worth spending some time and effort to find. I am also including in this chapter a few attractions which you may find worth seeking out, but which don't fit neatly into any of the tours or districts described previously.

GANSEN-JI
2-2-7 Daikoku, Naniwa-ku, Osaka (tel. 06-641-0084).

Gansen-ji, a small Zen temple tucked away beside a busy highway, conceals a little gem of a landscape garden behind its nondescript facade. Leave the Daikoku-chō subway station (Tanimachi or Yotsubashi Line) via Exit 5 and walk west along Route 25 for about two blocks. The temple gate is fairly obvious, but the entrance to the garden is quite obscure. Once inside the temple compound, turn right and look for a narrow, low passage under an enclosed walkway linking two buildings; the passage is about four feet high and closed by a wooden gate. There may be no signs of caretakers or resident monks about, so just open the gate and proceed into the garden beyond.

Gansen-ji's garden is in the style of the Muromachi period, and was likely constructed near the end of that period. The design carries an unsubstantiated attribution to Sōami, an early sixteenth-century painter and garden designer credited apocryphally with hundreds of garden designs in the Kinki region. The major elements of a Muromachi Zen garden are preserved here, though recent alterations are apparent, especially around its edges; the stone lantern is also a latter-day feature. The core of the garden is a splendid composition of rocks and plantings best viewed from the narrow veranda attached to the very ordinary two-story building that faces the garden.

IDEMITSU ART MUSEUM

3-4-26 Minami Semba, Chūō-ku (tel. 06-245-8611). 10 A.M. to 4:30 P.M. Closed Mondays, December 28 to January 4, and during exhibition installations. Admission: ¥100.

The Idemitsu Art Museum is one of Tokyo's leading private museums. Its recently opened Osaka branch is located on the thirteenth floor of the Idemitsu Nagahori Building. From Sony Tower (see the Shinsaibashi section, map 3) cross to the north side of Nagahori-dōri, the broad avenue which the Sony Tower faces, then walk two blocks east. The Idemitsu has a superb collection of Japanese, Chinese, and Korean art. The Osaka branch presents several shows annually, and there are frequent overseas exhibitions as well. Illustrated pamphlets and catalogues are available with English text.

ITSUŌ ART MUSEUM

7-17 Tateishi-chō, Ikeda-shi (tel. 0727-51-3865). 10 A.M. to 4:30 P.M. Closed Mondays and December 28 to January 4. Admission: ¥500.

The Itsuō Art Museum is less than 1 kilometer from the Hankyu Ikeda Station, but the route is a circuitous one up a suburban hillside, so take a taxi from the station. The collection was assembled by Kobayashi Ichizō, the founder of the Hankyu Railway. After his death in 1957, his house was converted into a gallery and opened to the public. The house is basically Western in style, and the remaining interior details are quite sumptuous. The whole is set in a Japanese garden which includes an elegant little tea garden you can stroll through. Later additions to the museum are unobtrusive. The collection itself is extensive, both broad and deep. It includes Japanese paintings and calligraphy; ceramics from Japan, China, Korea, and the West; and Chinese sculpture. Of five thousand or so objects in the collection, less than a hundred are on view at any one time. Exhibits change four times a year.

MUSEUMS AND ASSORTED MONUMENTS

KUBOSŌ MEMORIAL MUSEUM OF ARTS

85 Uchida-chō, Izumi-shi (tel. 0725-53-1071). 10 A.M. to 5 P.M. Closed Mondays, December 28 to January 4, and during February and August. Admission: ¥200. Teahouse open daily in April, May, and October; open on Thursdays from 11 A.M. to 3 P.M. year-round.

Probably the most difficult museum to reach of those listed here, the Kubosō Memorial Museum of Arts is also among the most attractive. Established in 1982, it is now considered one of Japan's finest small art museums. Take the JR Hanwa Line from Tennō-ji to Izumi-fuchū, then taxi or bus to Bijutsukan-mae (about 25 minutes by bus, slightly less by cab).

The museum is a long, low, tile-roofed structure designed by Takenaka Kōmuten in a rather traditional Japanese style. The building has a serene quality, and the large lounge that faces a lovely garden is an especially gracious room. A teahouse in the upper garden is open only for special occasions. Below, and across a bridge, is a larger building, also used primarily as a teahouse but open to the public at various times during the year. This building was constructed in 1941 in the traditional *sukiya shoin* style.

The collection, compiled by several generations of the wealthy Kubo family, concentrates on early Japanese painting, calligraphy, ceramics, and lacquer; it also includes Chinese paintings, ceramics, bronzes, and mirrors. The objects tend to be small and delicate, refined in the best sense of the word. Their most often reproduced painting is *Sparrow on a Branch* by Miyamoto Musashi (also known as Niten), the samurai swordsman whose book on military strategy was touted in the 1980s as the key to understanding Japanese business practices. Displays change five times a year.

MANNO ART MUSEUM

2-2-3 Shinsaibashi, Chūō-ku, Osaka (tel. 06-212-1517). 10 A.M. to 4:30 P.M., March 1 to July 31 and September 1 to December 31. Closed Mondays. Admission: ¥500.

Located on the thirteenth floor of an office building on the west side of Midōsuji, about three blocks south of the Daimaru department store, the entrance to the Manno Art Museum is identified by a pair of stone lions. Another private collection gone public, this museum has a number of excellent Tokugawa-period screen paintings, as well as a group of samurai accoutrements for the military historian. The quality of the collection overall is high, but it does contain some controversial pieces. The museum opened in 1988, and the display is immaculate.

MASAKI ART MUSEUM
2-9-26 Tadaokanaka, Tadaoka-chō, Senboku-gun (tel. 0725-21-6000). 10 A.M. to 4:30 P.M., March 15 to June 30 and September 15 to December 15. Closed Wednesdays. Admission: ¥300.

Tadaoka Station is on the Nankai main line south of Sakai. The route there is a 15-minute walk north to the Tadaoka Shrine, then northeast along a major boulevard. This is yet another collection put together by a single individual. Among the Japanese paintings is an excellent group from the Muromachi period. Japanese and Chinese ceramics are also well represented. Small and relatively inconvenient, I can recommend it only if you are a serious art lover.

NAMBAN CULTURE HALL
2-2-16 Nakatsu, Oyodo-ku, Osaka (tel. 06-451-0088). 10 A.M. to 4 P.M., May and November. Closed Mondays. Admission: free.

A peculiar little museum in an odd location, the Namban is particularly hard to reach due to the complicated and intimidating group of elevated rail and highway structures beside and above it. Find the stairs descending from the highway west of the Hankyu Nakatsu Station. When you reach street level, you are nearly there. The museum is readily identified as a nearly windowless concrete box. *Namban* means "southern barbarians" and is the term developed to refer to foreigners at the time of the introduction of Christianity in the late sixteenth century. The collection consists mainly of Christian icons and other religious items, as well as some paintings of exotic foreign subjects. Although the material is interesting, labels are sorely lacking, in Japanese as well as English, making it hard to derive much sense from the displays. The museum is open only two months each year.

OSAKA TEMMANGŪ
2-1-8 Tenjimbashi, Kita-ku.

Since it is one of Osaka's oldest and richest shrines, and the host to the city's most elaborate festival, I feel duty-bound to include Osaka Temmangū in my text. You should not feel similarly obligated to visit, however. But if you wish to, you can reach it by walking south a few blocks from the Minami Morimachi subway station until you see a large torii on the east side of the street. Walk through it and continue east a few more blocks.

The shrine was established in 645 and became a Temmangū shrine (one dedicated to the deified statesman/poet Sugawara no Michizane) in 949. The current buildings are of no great distinction. The possible exception is the Ningyō-kan, a modern structure displaying scenes from the life of Michizane using dolls in diorama settings, which is unique if thoroughly unattractive. Those involved in academic pursuits may wish to buy *ema* (votive tablets) to enlist the aid of the patron deity—Michizane's assistance is desperately sought after by Japanese students taking the entrance exams that will determine their futures.

YAYOI MUSEUM
443-1 Ikegami-chō, Izumi-shi. 10 A.M. to 5 P.M. Closed Mondays. Admission is charged.

Take the JR Hanwa Line to Shinodayama Station, then walk west through a lovely old neighborhood for 15 minutes until you reach Route 26.

MUSEUMS AND ASSORTED MONUMENTS

The museum will be visible on the west side of the highway. The Yayoi Museum is dedicated to displays of Japan's prehistoric cultures, principally the Yayoi, but also the Jōmon and Tumulus periods. This is a very stylish new museum, probably the best design to date by the Prefectural Building Department's architecture staff. The exhibits include pottery and other artifacts, but also well-done reconstructions and some high-tech gizmos, most notably a village model which you can inspect up close by using remote-controlled video cameras.

YOSHIMURA RESIDENCE

5-3 Shimaizumi, Habikino (tel. 0729-54-8022). 10 A.M. to 4 P.M. on Sundays and national holidays. By appointment only. Admission: ¥300.

This building is a 5-minute taxi ride from Fujiidera Station on the Kintetsu Minami Osaka Line. The Yoshimura house is considered by many to be Japan's finest remaining example of a Tokugawa farmhouse (*minka*). Built around 1620, the house is unusually large, opulent, and exquisitely crafted, reflecting the wealth and status of its owners. Set in a simple courtyard, the house makes a powerful impression with its long gabled roof covered in a mix of thatch and tile. The carpentry work within is equally impressive, and the house as a whole is beautiful in such a homey way as to induce nostalgia for a time and a way of life which is truly beyond our comprehension.

As important personages in their farming community, the Yoshimura family would have received occasional visits from samurai in the local government. A dozen or so meters to the left of the main entrance is another entrance, this one more elaborate, with its own distinct roof above. This space is a *genkan,* and its use was (in theory at least) restricted to members of the samurai class. In this way, the VIP guests were spared the unpleasantness of passing by the family's living quarters and could be ushered directly into the formal rooms. Although the Yoshimura Residence is available for visits only by appointment, and only during certain seasons, it is more than sufficient reward for the effort.

MUSEUMS AND ASSORTED MONUMENTS

YUKI ART MUSEUM

3-3-9 Hirano-chō, Chūō-ku, Osaka (tel. 06-203-0188). Call for dates of exhibitions. 10 A.M. to 4 P.M. Closed Mondays. Admission: ¥500.

Head south for five blocks from the southeast exit of Yodoyabashi Station on the Midōsuji Line. At the Tōkai Building turn east and go two blocks more. The Yuki Art Museum displays material collected by the owner of Osaka's priciest *kaiseki* restaurant, Kitchō. The holdings are all related to the tea ceremony, and include many excellent pieces. Four exhibitions of selections from the collection are held each year.

FESTIVALS

Exhaustive calendars include as many as seventy-five annual festivals in the city of Osaka. I have selected the most popular and most impressive.

TŌKA EBISU   January 9 to 11, Imamiya Ebisu Shrine, 1-6-10 Ebisu-nishi, Naniwa-ku. Ebisu, the deity of prosperity and guardian of Osaka's merchants, is honored in this festival, which draws as many as a million visitors each year. An impressive procession of maidens in palanquins takes place on January 10.

DOYA-DOYA   January 14, Shitennō-ji. This is a "naked festival," in which two teams of youths, clad only in loincloths, compete for possession of a sacred amulet. Splashed with water, shoved about, and chanting "doya, doya" ("How are you?" in Osaka dialect), the participants are said to experience spiritual renewal and purification.

SHŌRYŌ-E   April 22, Shitennō-ji. This festival celebrates the anniversary of the death of Prince Shōtoku with a daytime procession, followed by evening performances of Bugaku dancing.

KAMIGATA HANABUTAI   Late May, National Bunraku Theater. Not truly a festival, this annual event is considered the year's premier Bunraku performance.

OTAUE-SHINJI   June 14, Sumiyoshi Taisha. The rice-planting festival (see description on page 74).

AIZEN MATSURI   June 30 to July 2, Shōman-in (see map 4). Processions of young women in palanquins and young men dressed in *yukata* (cotton kimono), plus *yamabushi* (mountain priests) building a sacred fire, create a noisy, bustling spectacle.

FESTIVALS

DANJIRI MATSURI July 12 to 13, Kumata Jinja, Hirano (see map 5). A *danjiri* is a portable wooden shrine, elaborately carved and decorated in gilding, braided tassels, and paper lanterns, with a "porch" on the front where seated musicians perform. The shrines are pulled through the streets, carrying their Shinto deities into the neighborhoods. Competitions take place between teams, each pulling a danjiri, in the area around Kumata Jinja. The festival is popular, with up to three hundred thousand visitors, and a little dangerous, as the massive shrines are pulled forward and backward, sometimes at high speeds, along the crowded streets.

TENJIN MATSURI July 24 to 25, Nakanoshima to Sakuranomiya, and Osaka Temmangū shrine. As the venue suggests, this is a huge and spectacular festival, Osaka's largest and most beautiful. It celebrates the rivers which have been central to Osaka's historical development. The festival, which dates back to the tenth century, features a procession from the Temmangū shrine to Tenjin-bashi. The floats, portable shrines, and participants then move out onto the Okawa River in boats on the evening of July 25. Torchlit boats, including elaborate dragon boats, take part in an event which is part parade, part race, accompanied by spectacular fireworks. Crowds are mammoth.

KAGARI NO BUGAKU August 8, Shitennō-ji. Bugaku is performed by torchlight on the temple grounds.

TAKIGI NOH August 11 to 12, Ikutama Jinja, 13-9 Ikutama-chō, Tennōji-ku. Noh plays are performed by torchlight at the shrine in a sort of sequel to Shitennō-ji's Bugaku dances.

KISHIWADA DANJIRI MATSURI September 14 to 15, and repeated on October 9 to 10, Kishiwada city (20 minutes south from Namba on the Nankai Line). This is the most famous and raucous of the area's danjiri festivals (see above). The fighting among the rival teams is intense, as floats collide and their riders try to invade the other vehicles. Injuries to participants and spectators are common, occasionally resulting in fatalities.

MIDŌSUJI PARADE Early October, Midōsuji Street. A curious East-meets-West event, with marching bands and drill teams, Southeast Asian dancers, and portable Shinto shrines.

SHINNŌ-SAI November 22 to 23, Sakunahikona Shrine, 2-1-8 Doshō-machi, Chūō-ku. Originating with a cholera outbreak in 1822, the festival is thought to protect against disease. Paper tiger talismans are given out in commemoration of medicines developed by the local herbalists and packaged in paper tigers at the time of the 1822 epidemic. Sakunahikona Shrine is dedicated to the god of herbal medicine, and is located in the traditional pharmaceutical district of Osaka.

USEFUL KANJI

INSIDE THE LOOP
UNDERGROUND UMEDA

DŌJIMA	堂島
EKIMAE	駅前
HANKYŪ	阪急
HANSHIN	阪神
MIDŌSUJI	御堂筋
OHATSU-TENJIN-DŌRI	お初天神通り
SONEZAKI	曾根崎
TANIMACHI	谷町
UMEDA	梅田
YOTSUBASHI	四つ橋

OSAKA CASTLE AND VICINITY

ENSHŌ-GURA	焔硝蔵
HONMARU	本丸
INUI TURRET	乾櫓
NANIWA PALACE	難波宮
NISHINOMARU	西の丸
OSAKA CASTLE	大阪城
OSAKA CITY MUSEUM	大阪市立博物館
OSAKA-JŌ KŌEN	大阪城公園
ŌTE-MON	大手門
SAKURA-MON	桜門
SENGAN TURRET	千貫櫓
TAMON TURRET	多聞櫓

THE RIVERFRONTS

BANK OF JAPAN	日本銀行大阪支店
FUJITA MUSEUM OF ART	藤田美術館
HIGO-BASHI	肥後橋

USEFUL KANJI

KAWASAKI-BASHI	川崎橋
MUSEUM OF ORIENTAL CERAMICS	東洋陶器美術館
NAKANOSHIMA	中之島
NAKANOSHIMA CENTRAL HALL	中之島中央公会堂
NANIWA-BASHI	難波橋
OSAKA MINT	大蔵省造幣局
OSAKA PREFECTURAL LIBRARY	大阪府立中之島図書館
OSAKA SCIENCE MUSEUM	大阪市立科学館
SAKURANOMIYA	桜之宮
SEMPU-KAN	泉布観
SUISHŌ-BASHI	水晶橋
TEKIJUKU	適塾
TENJIN-BASHI	天神橋
YODOYA-BASHI	淀屋橋

OSAKA BUSINESS PARK

KYŌBASHI	京橋

SHINSAIBASHI

SHINSAIBASHI	心斎橋

NAMBA

DŌTOMBORI	道頓堀
HŌZEN-JI	法善寺
JAPAN FOLK ART MUSEUM	日本工芸館
NAMBA	難波
NATIONAL BUNRAKU THEATER	国立文楽劇場
NEW KABUKI THEATER	新歌舞伎座

SHITENNŌ-JI

SHITENNŌ-JI	四天王寺
STONE TORII	石の鳥居

UEMACHI RIDGE

AIZEN-ZAKA	愛染坂

USEFUL KANJI

GAKUEN-ZAKA	学園坂
GENSHŌJI-ZAKA	源聖寺坂
IKUTAMA JINJA	生国魂神社
ISSHIN-JI	一心寺
KIYOMIZU-DERA	清水寺
KUCHINAWA-ZAKA	口縄坂
SHŌMAN-IN	勝髪院
TENJIN-ZAKA	天神坂
UEMACHI RIDGE	上町大地

TENNŌ-JI

KEITAKU-EN	慶沢園
MUNICIPAL MUSEUM OF ART	大阪市立美術館
SHIN-SEKAI	新世界
TENNŌ-JI	天王寺
TENNŌ-JI ZOO	天王寺動物園
TSŪTENKAKU	通天閣

OUTSIDE THE LOOP

SUMIYOSHI

HANKAI STREETCAR LINE	阪堺電軌
IKUNE JINJA	生根神社
NANKAI LINE	南海電鉄
ŌAMA JINJA	大海神社
OTAUE-SHINJI	お田植神社
SUMIYOSHI TAISHA	住吉大社
HIRANO	平野
DAINEMBUTSU-JI	大念仏寺

HIRANO

KAMI STATION	加美駅
KUMATA JINJA	杭全神社
OKUDA HOUSE	奥田家住宅

USEFUL KANJI

SANJŪBU JINJA	三十歩神社
SENKŌ-JI	全興寺
YAMATOJI LINE	大和寺線

SAKAI AND VICINITY

DAISEN KŌEN	大仙公園
HAMADERA	浜寺
HANWA LINE	阪和線
MIKUNIGAOKA STATION	三国ヶ丘駅
MOZU STATION	百舌鳥駅
NINTOKU'S TUMULUS	仁徳天皇陵
ŌTORI TAISHA	大鳥大社
SAKAI	堺市

TONDABAYASHI CITY

JINAI-MACHI	寺内町
NISHIKIORI JINJA	錦織神社
RYŪSEN-JI	龍泉寺
SUGIYAMA RESIDENCE	旧杉山家住宅
TONDABAYASHI	富田林

KAWACHI NAGANO

AMAMI STATION	天見駅
(AMANOSAN) KONGŌ-JI	(天野山)金剛寺
ENMEI-JI	延命寺
KAMI-KOBUKA	上小深
KANSHIN-JI	観心寺
KAWACHI NAGANO	河内長野
MANI-IN	摩尼院
MIKKAICHICHŌ STATION	三日市町駅
NANKAI KŌYA LINE	南海高野線
OKUDEN	奥殿
TAKIHATA	滝畑
YAMAMOTO RESIDENCE	山本家住宅

USEFUL KANJI

OSAKA HARBOR

OSAKA AQUARIUM	大阪海遊館
BENTEN-CHŌ	弁天町
NISHIKU-JŌ STATION	西九条駅
OSAKA HARBOR	大阪港
TEMPŌZAN	天保山

NATURE

PARKS

BOTANICAL GARDEN	植物園
EXPO PARK	万博公園
HATTORI RYOKUCHI KŌEN	服部緑地公園
INTERNATIONAL INSTITUTE FOR CHILDREN'S LITERATURE	国際児童文学館
JAPAN FOLK CRAFTS MUSEUM	日本民芸館
KYŌBASHI	京橋
MUSEUM OF JAPANESE FARM-HOUSES	日本民家集落博物館
NATIONAL MUSEUM OF ETHNOLOGY	国立民族学博物館
OSAKA NATIONAL MUSEUM OF ART	国立国際美術館
SENRI CHŪŌ	千里中央
TSURUMI RYOKUCHI KŌEN	鶴見緑地公園

ESCAPING THE CITY

FUMIN NO MORI	府民の森
HIRAOKA	枚岡
KATSUO-JI	勝尾寺
KITA SENRI	北千里
MINOO	箕面市
MT. IKOMA	生駒山

USEFUL KANJI

NAKAFUTŌ	中埠頭
NANKŌ YACHŌ KŌEN	南港野鳥公園
NARUKAWA ENCHI	なるかわ園地

DINING, SHOPPING, AND MORE
DINING

AJI-BIL	あじびる
BOTEJYŪ	ぼてぢゅう
FUKAMOTO	ふかもと
HIDEYOSHI	秀吉
HONJIN	本陣
ICHIRIKI	市力
ISARIBI	漁火
KANI DORAKU	かに道楽
KAZOKU-TEI	家族亭
KITCHŌ	吉兆
MARUMAN HONKE	丸萬本家
NISHIKE	にし家
SHIRUKIYO	しる清
SHŌBENTANGO-TEI	正弁丹吾亭
SUMO CHAYA	角力茶屋
TAIKŌ-EN	太閤園
TAKOUME	たこ梅

BOOKSTORES AND SPECIALTY SHOPPING

ASAHIYA	旭屋
DŌGUYA-SUJI	道具屋筋
INTERNATIONAL MARKET	国際市場
KINOKUNIYA	紀伊国屋
KOSHO-NO-MACHI	古書の町
KUROMON	黒門
MARUZEN	丸善
MATCHAMACHI-SUJI	松屋町筋

USEFUL KANJI

TACHIBANA-DŌRI	立花通り
TENGYŪ	天牛
TSURUHASHI	鶴橋

MUSEUMS AND ASSORTED MONUMENTS

GANSEN-JI	願泉寺
IDEMITSU ART MUSEUM	出光美術館
ITSUŌ ART MUSEUM	逸翁美術館
KUBOSŌ MEMORIAL MUSEUM OF ARTS	久保惣記念美術館
MANNO ART MUSEUM	萬屋美術館
MASAKI ART MUSEUM	正木美術館
NAMBAN CULTURE HALL	南蛮文化館
OSAKA TEMMANGŪ	大阪天満宮
YAYOI MUSEUM	弥生博物館
YOSHIMURA RESIDENCE	吉村家住宅
YUKI ART MUSEUM	湯木美術館

INDEX

Academy Travel and Used Books 135
ACTY Osaka 15
Aizen-dō 50
Aji-Bil Restaurants 127
Amami Onsen and Station 98, 99
Amanosan Kongō-ji (see: Kongō-ji)
Amerika Mura 37–38
Andō Tadao 36–37, 51–52
Aqualiner 23
Asahiya Bookstore 133
Asuka period 5, 46

Bank of Japan 29
Banpaku Kinen Kōen (Expo Park)
    109–112, 113; Expoland 112;
    International Institute for Children's Literature 111, 113; Japan
    Folkcrafts Museum 111, 113;
    National Museum of Ethnology
    111, 113; Osaka National
    Museum of Art 111, 113
Bara Teien 83–84
Benten-chō Passenger Terminal 101
Buddhism 5, 6, 45–47, 76, 87, 89,
    90, 94, 96
Bugaku Dance 47, 48
Bunraku 11, 41–42, 145
Business Hotel Ohtani 130

Capsule Hotel Asahi Plaza Shinsaibashi 130
Chikamatsu Monzaemon 11, 41, 42, 132
Children's Museum 37
Country Life Restaurant 125

D/A Brasserie 125
D-Hotel 130
Daimaru Department Store 35
Dainembutsu-ji 76
Daisen Kōen 81, 82, 84
Den-den Town (Electronics District) 137
Diamond Trail 99
Dōguya-suji (Kitchen Utensil Street) 136
Dōjima River 30
Dōjima Shopping Arcade 15
Dōtombori 38, 39, 40, 41

Ebisu-sō Ryokan 130
Edo period (see Tokugawa period)
Enmei-ji 98
Expo Park (see: Banpaku Kinen Kōen)
Expoland 112

Festivals 145–147; Bugaku 48, 145,
    146; Otaue-Shinji 74, 145
Flea Markets 75, 135
Fujita Museum of Art 27, 28, 32, 125
Fumin no Mori 114–116

Gansen-ji 138
Go-Daigo, Emperor 91, 92, 95, 98
Go-Murakami, Emperor 92, 93, 94

Hamadera Kōen 83–85, 107
Hankai streetcar line 51, 71
Hankyu Railway 12, 116, 134;
    Umeda Station 132
Hankyu Sanbangai 13, 14, 123

INDEX

Hanshin Mall 14, 15
Hanshin Railway 12; Umeda Station 15
Hattori Ryokuchi Kōen 98, 107, 113, 128
Hattori Youth Hostel 128
Heian period 48, 97
Hideyoshi 6, 7, 11, 17–20, 50, 73, 75, 79
Hideyoshi Restaurant 124
Higashi Umeda Station 11, 15
Hirano 76–78
Hiraoka Jinja 114–115
Hokkō 100, 103
Holiday Inn Nankai-Osaka 130
Honjin Bar 124
Hotel New Otani Osaka 129
Hotel Nikko Osaka 130
Hōzen-ji 40, 126

Ichiriki Restaurant 124
Idemitsu Art Museum 139
Ikune Jinja 75
Imperial Hotel (Teikoku Hoteru) 130
International Flower and Greenery Exposition 8, 112
International Institute for Children's Literature 111, 113
International Market 136–137
International Market Place 34
Isaribi Restaurant 123–124
Ishii Osamu 127
Ishiyama Hongan-ji 6, 18, 77, 86
Isshin-ji 49
Itsuō Art Museum 139

Jan-Jan Yokochō 53
Japan Folk Art Museum 43, 44
Japan Folk Crafts Museum 111, 113

Japan Railways (JR) loop line 8, 23, 25, 51, 53, 71, 102
Jimmu, Emperor 4
Jinai-machi 86–88; Museum 87, 88
Jingū, Empress 72–73, 74
Jōmon period 4, 143
JR Hanwa Line 79, 82, 139, 142
JR Yamatoji Line 76

Kabuki 41
Kaitokudō 7
Kamakura period 90
Kani Dōraku Restaurant 39, 123, 126
Kansai International Airport 100, 103
Kanshin-ji 95–98, 99; Kondō 96, 98; Nyoirin Kannon 97; Tatekake-no-tō 98
Katsuo-ji 117
Kawachi Nagano 89–99, 130; Youth Hostel 130
Kawasaki Kiyoshi 111
Kawasaki-bashi 27
Keitaku-en 52
Kikutake Kiyonori 109
Kinokuniya Bookstore 132
Kintetsu Line 51; Nagano Line 86; Nara Line 114
Kirin Plaza 36, 39
Kitchō Restaurant 123, 124, 129, 144
Kiyomizu-dera and Kiyomizu-zaka 50
Kōbō Daishi (Kūkai) 89–90, 94, 95
Kofun period 4, 81, 143
Kongō-Ikoma Quasi-National Park 114, 115
Kongō-ji 89–95, 97, 98, 99, 130; Hōmotsukan 94; Kondō 94; Mani-in 93; Okuden 92, 93; Shōmon 94; Tahōtō 94

Kosho-no-machi (Old Book Town) 134
Kubosō Memorial Museum of Arts 140
Kūkai (see: Kōbō Daishi)
Kumata Jinja 76–77, 146
Kurokawa Kishō 35, 36, 42–43, 111
Kuromon (Produce Market) 137
Kusunoki Masashige 91, 95, 98
Kyoto vii, viii, 6, 72, 90, 91

Love Suicides at Sonezaki 11, 42

Machiya (townhouses) 29, 30, 31, 87
Manno Art Museum 140–141
Maruman Honke Restaurant 126
Maruzen Bookstore 133
Masaki Art Museum 141
Matchamachi-suji (Toy District) 137
Meiji era vii, 24, 27, 28
Meiji no Mori Minoo Quasi-National Park (see: Minoo Park)
Meiji Restoration 7, 19, 24, 28, 117
Midōsuji Line 13, 133; Umeda Station 13, 14
Midōsuji Street 35, 37, 38, 43, 133, 141, 147
Mikkaichichō 98
Minka (farmhouses) 98, 108, 143
Minoo Park 116–117; Minoo Park Visitors' Center 116, 118
Mizukake Fudō 40
Modern Transportation Museum 102, 104
Momoyama period 75
Moti Restaurant 126
Mount Ikoma 114, 115
Mount Iwawaki 99

Mount Kōya (Kōya-san) 27, 90, 97, 98
Murano Tōgō 35, 43
Muromachi period 76, 77, 79, 95, 138
Museum of Oriental Ceramics 28, 29, 32

Nakanoshima 11, 15, 23, 24, 27–32, 83, 129, 146; Nakanoshima Central Hall 28; Kōen 27, 107
Namba 39–44, 51, 53, 71, 79, 84, 89, 125, 130
Namban Culture Hall 141–142
Nambokuchō period 90–93, 94, 98
Naniwa 4
Naniwa Palace 5, 6, 19, 22
Naniwa-bashi 28
Nankai City Mall 44
Nankai Line 51, 71, 79; Hamadera Station 84; Kōya Line 84, 89, 98
Nankō 103, 107, 117
Nankō Yachō Kōen (Nanko Wild Bird Sanctuary) 103, 117–118
Nara vii, 5, 45, 91
Nara period 87
Narukawa Enchi 114, 115
National Bunraku Theater 39, 41, 42–43, 44
National Living Plaza 33, 34
National Museum of Ethnology 111, 113
New Kabuki Theater 43, 44
New Osaka Hotel 128
Nikken Sekkei 29, 34
Nintoku, Emperor 4, 80; Burial Mound 79–81
Nishike Restaurant 125
Nishikiori Jinja 87

INDEX

Noguchi Magoichi 28
Noh 41

Ōama Jinja 75
Oda Nobunaga 6, 17, 18, 77
Oda Sakunosuke 40, 132, 133
Ogata Kōan 29–31
Ohatsu Tenjin 11
Ohatsu-tenjin-dōri 12
Oimatsu-dōri (Garō-dōri; Gallery Street) 135
Ōjin, Emperor 73, 80
Okada Shin'ichirō 28
Okuda House 78
Open-air Museum of Japanese Farmhouses 108–109
Osaka Aquarium viii, 100, 103
Osaka Bay 3, 4, 20, 47
Osaka Business Park 17, 19, 33–34, 121, 129
Osaka Castle 3, 5, 8, 17, 19–23, 33; Enshō-gura 21; Honmaru 21, 22; Inui Turret 21; Nishi no maru 21; Ōte-mon 20; Sakura-mon 21; Sengan Turret 20, 21; Tamon Turret 20, 21
Osaka Castle Hotel 129
Osaka Central Post Office 15
Osaka City Museum 19, 22, 23
Osaka City Hall 29
Osaka Corona Hotel 128
Osaka Ekimae Buildings 15
Osaka Foundation of International Exchange 121
Osaka Harbor 100–104
Osaka Hilton 129
Osaka International House 121
Osaka Mint 23, 24, 25–26; Museum 26, 32

Osaka Municipal Museum of Art 51, 52, 54
Osaka National Museum of Art 111, 113
Osaka Prefectural Library 28
Osaka Resort City 102
Osaka Science Museum 30–32
Osaka Station 12, 15, 121, 129
Osaka Summer War 7, 18
Osaka Temmangū Shrine 142, 146
Osaka Terminal Hotel 15, 129
Osaka-jō Hall 22
Osaka-jō Kōen 22, 107
Ōtori Taisha 74, 82–83

Panasonic Square 33, 34
Paradiso 102, 103, 104
Peace Tower 87–88
Piano, Renzo 103
Pig and Whistle Pub 126
Puchishan Mall 13, 14

Royal Hotel 129
Ryūan-ji 116
Ryūsen-ji 87

Sakai 4, 74, 79–85; City Museum 81, 84
Sakuranomiya Park 24, 25, 26
Sakuranomiya-bashi 25, 27
Second World War viii, 7, 27, 46, 49, 53, 73, 91
Sen no Rikyū 18, 79
Senkō-ji 77–78
Sempu-kan 25, 26, 32
Shin-Osaka 128; Station 121
Shin-Osaka Washington Hotel 128
Shin-Sekai 52–53
Shinji-gawa 11

INDEX

Shinsaibashi 35–37, 39, 42, 53, 125, 130, 139; Station 35
Shinsaibashi-suji 35, 36, 39
Shinto 47, 71, 73–75, 77, 82, 115
Shirukiyo Restaurant 125
Shitennō-ji 3, 5, 8, 45–48, 49, 97; Festivals 145, 146; Flea Market 135; Gochikō-in 47; Kodō 46; Kondō 46; Pagoda 46; Rokuji-dō 47; Torii 46–47
Shōbentango-tei Restaurant 40, 126
Shōman-in 50, 145
Shōtoku, Prince (Shōtoku Taishi) 5, 45, 47, 77, 89
Sōgō Department Store 35
Sony Tower 35, 36, 42, 139
Sugiyama Residence 86–87, 88
Suiko, Empress 45
Suishō-bashi 29
Suma 72
Sumiyoshi district 71–75; Kōen 71, 107
Sumiyoshi Taisha 5, 71–75, 82; Flea Market 75, 135
Sumo Chaya Restaurant 126

Tachibana-dori (Furniture Wholesale Street) 137
Taikō-en Restaurant 27, 125
Takaguchi Yasuyuki 49
Takamatsu Shin 36, 39
Takemoto Gidayū 41
Takenaka Kōmuten 34, 140
Takeyama Sei 130
Taki Mitsuo 108
Takihata Reservoir 99
Takoume Restaurant 40, 126
Tatsuno Kingo 29
Tekijuku 29–31, 32

Teku Teku Road 79
Temmabashi Station 17, 133
Temmu, Emperor 5
Tempōzan 100–102; Ferry Terminal 101; Harbor Village 100; Kōen 100; Marketplace 102
Tengyū Bookstore 133–134
Tennō-ji 51–54, 79; Station 76
Tennō-ji Park 49, 51–52, 54, 107; Keitaku-en 52; Osaka Municipal Museum of Art 51, 52, 54; Tennō-ji Zoo 52, 54
Toilets of the World 34
Tōkai Shizen Hodō (Tōkai Nature Trail) 117
Tokio Marine and Fire Insurance Building 34
Tokugawa Ieyasu 6, 18
Tokugawa period vii, 7, 19, 20, 24, 30, 47, 50, 76, 77, 100, 116, 132, 136, 141
Tokyo vii, viii, 30, 35, 132
Tondabayashi City 86–88
Toyotomi Hideyoshi (see Hideyoshi)
Tsu-no-kuni 5, 45
Tsurumi Ryokuchi Kōen 112, 113
Tsūtenkaku 53, 54
Tumulus period (see Kofun period)
Twin Towers 33

Uemachi Ridge 3, 5, 47, 49–50
Umeda 11–16, 24, 40, 51, 116, 129, 132, 133, 134
Umeda OS Hotel 129
Urabe Shizutarō 43

Wakabayashi Hiroyuki 37
Whity Mall 14, 16; Whity East 13; Whity North 14; Whity South 15

INDEX

World Exposition of 1970 8, 109, 110, 111

Yamamoto family farmhouse 98
Yamato River 3
Yasui Jinja 49
Yayoi Museum 142

Yayoi period 4, 143
Yodo River 3, 25, 26, 100
Yodoya Jōan 24
Yōroppa Mura 37
Yoshimura Residence 143
Yoshino 91, 97
Yuki Art Museum 143

The "weathermark" identifies this book as a production of Weatherhill, Inc., publishers of fine books on Asia and the Pacific. Editorial supervision: Meg Taylor. Book design and typography: Liz Trovato. Production supervision: Bill Rose. Text composition: G & H SOHO, Inc., Hoboken, New Jersey. Color separations: ISCOA, Arlington, Virginia. Printing and binding, Arcata Graphics, Fairfield, Pennsylvania. The typeface used is Frutiger 47 light condensed.